Architect's
Essentials of
Professional
Development

Other Titles in the Architect's Essentials of Professional Practice Series:

Architect's Essentials of Ownership Transition
   Peter Piven with William Mandel

Architect's Essentials of Cost Management
   Michael Dell'Isola

Architect's Essentials of Contract Negotiation
   Ava Abramowitz

Architect's Essentials of Presentation Skills
   David Greusel

Architect's Essentials of Starting a Design Firm
   Peter Piven and Bradford Perkins

Architect's Essentials of Winning Proposals
   Frank A. Stasiowski

Architect's Essentials of Professional Development

Jean R. Valence

WILEY

John Wiley & Sons, Inc.

Library of Congress Cataloging-in-Publication Data:

Valence, Jean R.
   Architect's essentials of professional development / Jean R. Valence.
       p. cm. — (The architect's essentials of professional practice)
   Includes index.
       ISBN 0-471-23691-8 (pbk. : alk. paper)
       1. Architects—In-service training. 2. Architecture—Study and teaching. 3. Architectural firms—Management. I. Title. II. Architect's essentials of professional practice series.
   NA1996.V35 2003
   720'.71'5—dc21
                                                    2003002098

To Phil, who changed my life.

Contents

8
Implementation

9
Evaluation

10
Learning from Learning

APPENDIX
Suggested Learning Objectives for Architect's Essentials of Professional Development

Foreword

Professional development, or continuing education as it is commonly labeled these days, has become a very distinct and important part of an architect's daily professional life.

Over the last few years, the architecture profession has witnessed a proliferation of confusing and disparate continuing education requirements; and we have all participated in a wide variety of educational activities: courses, magazine quizzes, seminars and tours, some of excellent value and others very disappointing. Fortunately, in *Architect's Essentials of Professional Development*, Jean Valence brings structure and rigor to various systems for professional development across North America.

For those architects still skeptical of the need for a structured system of continuing education, this book will convince them. Valence does not dwell on the establishment of continuing education requirements by regulators to ensure the architecture profession remains current and competent in matters of health, safety, and welfare. Instead, she argues that professional development provides a "competitive edge" for firms and individual architects. Professional development is simply good business!

This book is an indispensable guide for architecture firms that want to establish a coherent and structured program for professional development. In addition, it is helpful to others, such as owners and developers involved in delivering and maintaining building projects, AIA/CES providers, and Canadian provincial associations that develop and deliver continuing education to architects. The book also provides suggestions geared to individual architects, as outlined in the intriguing appendix to each chapter called "Mavericks and Sole Proprietors."

In order for a successful, permanent continuing education program to flourish, it is necessary for any organization to develop a strategic plan to guide the program. *Architect's Essentials of Professional Development* outlines the steps to take, from strategic principles through implementation and evaluation, in order to make such a program happen. Valence's clear, sequential guidance, chapter by chapter, is reinforced by the inclusion of "learning objectives" for each chapter—a device to motivate readers to think in the right direction about professional development.

Valence is a management consultant, who has also chaired the AIA/CES Awards jury. I was fortunate to work with her as a member of two of these juries. At first I wondered how she could evaluate professional development for architects; I soon discovered that she brings a refreshing "organizational" perspective to the topic of professional development. As chairperson, Valence was able to guide the CES Awards jury toward the appropriate recognition of excellence in continuing education *systems* for architects. Valence's ability to seek out and find excellence is also demonstrated in this book, in which we learn what many outstanding architecture firms are doing in this realm. The book contains numerous examples; several award-winning architecture firms describe how they implemented a professional development program. The book also contains numerous case studies, examples, and quotations that demonstrate the validity of Valence's theories. These examples ground the book and provide the reader with a sense of reality.

This book deserves the attention of all design professionals, especially those involved in the establishment and regulation of professional development programs.

Jon Hobbs, MRAIC, Assoc. AIA

Acknowledgments

I am greatly indebted to the resourceful and visionary people and firms that were among the first to create powerful learning programs for their organizations and to the thoughtful "mavericks" who contributed to the development of this book.

I thank Thom Lowther, Ed.S., director of the AIA Continuing Education System, who has crafted a remarkable organization for professional development and knowledge-sharing for AIA members. In addition to sharing a little of his considerable expertise about the "Architect's Educational Universe" in this book, Thom introduced me to innovative firm leaders and education specialists, and encouraged me to test many of my planning models in the CES Leadership Summits.

I am somewhat grateful to wonderful author Andy Pressman, FAIA, who suggested that I address this topic and who makes writing look painless, which indeed it is not. My thanks to John Wiley editor Margaret Cummins, who invited me to write about professional development for *The Architect's Essentials* series and who guided me with patience, humor, and grace. I am indebted to educator Jeffrey Valence, who translated scribbles into 13 clear figures; and grateful to Gary Moyer AIA, for creating a coherent timeline from a pathetic fax. I thank Bonnie Sloan, FSMPS, whose editorial suggestions were, as usual, excellent. I thank Phil Valence, my husband and Blackridge partner, for his support, advice, and feedback on this book, and for covering for me with our clients as deadlines approached.

Above all, I thank the design professionals with whom I have worked for 25 years. I admire the way they think, the things they do, and the way they get things done for the benefit of us all.

Competitive Edge

"When I received my architectural degree, I regarded it as a license to learn. I still do."

So stated Charles Redmon, FAIA, a principal of Cambridge Seven Associates in Massachusetts, responding to a question posed at a brainstorming session at the Boston Architectural Center (BAC). One of the nation's oldest and largest schools of architecture, the BAC was hosting a board of directors' planning retreat, and the inquirer wanted to know what architects liked best about professional practice.

Whether architects begin their careers with a powerful curiosity and appetite for knowledge or whether they acquire the taste through the experience of serving clients and completing a range of commissions, most design professionals share Redmon's attitude. Practice is dynamic. Every day architects acquire new insights during the process of serving clients. The desire to enhance people's physical surroundings, and the responsibility for protecting the public health, safety, and welfare, demand professional growth. New information and ideas continually surge through professional practice.

In recent years in America, consciousness among architects about continuing education has heightened, as a result both of a wave of state initiatives requiring continuing education for architect registration and of the American Institute of Architects' (AIA's) adoption of a continuing education requirement for all members. Combined with a preference for knowledge and a need to address ever-changing client needs, this new sense of urgency has riveted attention on lifelong learning.

From the perspective of both the individual practitioner and the design firm, the most beneficial place for the professional's continuing education is professional practice itself. Architects seem to prefer organic learning that is acquired in the context of practice, particularly during projects, and to rely on firms as their primary source for learning (Price 1997). Firms are quickly learning what corporate America has known for a long time: that staff development is good business.

Former Royal Dutch/Shell executive Arie de Geus was a pioneer in organizational learning, and his work inspires organizational experts, Peter Senge among them. During his career at Shell, de Geus and his colleagues became intrigued with long-lived companies, particularly those not family-owned. Pulp and paper manufacturer Stora had begun as a copper mine in the 1300s. Hudson's Bay Company, Canada's largest department store retailer, hails its 300-year-old fur trading origins. Two centuries ago, Du Pont was making gunpowder.

De Geus's observations about businesses that survive for centuries, "living" companies, seem particularly appropriate for architecture firms. As he explained in his book, *The Living Company* (1997), people who want their organization to thrive should imbue it with four capabilities: "the ability to learn and adapt," "the ability to build a community and persona for itself," "the ability to build constructive relationships with other entities, within and outside itself," and "the ability to govern its own growth." All of these capabilities emerge from learning.

Research conducted by the American Institute of Architects in its AIA Firm Survey 2000–2001 shows that almost 30 percent of design firms provide in-house continuing education for staff. Almost 75 percent of firms with more than 10 people have internal continuing education programs. Even sole practitioners are capturing the learning potential of practice, with 7 percent reporting on-site professional development (American Institute of Architects, 2001).

Key Point

Firms, or individuals, that adopt a deliberate approach to learning sharpen their competitive edge in the marketplace for the long term.

The purpose of *Architect's Essentials of Professional Development* is to help registered architects design their own professional development approach and program, because tapping the knowledge wellspring of practice enhances practice itself. Firms, or individuals, that adopt a deliberate approach to learning sharpen their competitive edge in the marketplace for the long term.

Competitive Edge and Professional Development

Design firms constantly compete with each other for projects and people, and the ability of a firm to demonstrate its unique contribution to clients and staff is critical to its success. A professional development program, designed by and for the firm, can and should advance the firm's distinct attributes. It should:

> Feed the firm's accumulation of knowledge.

> Stimulate business excellence.

> Inspire innovation and fresh ideas among its staff.

> Reinforce the firm's culture.

Accumulating Knowledge

Learning is such an integral aspect of the design process that architects are typically unaware of the remarkable amount of qualitative and quantitative information and insight they accumulate during each project. Over and over again, architects study a client's world, conduct research, and synthesize data and ideas so that they can create a solution uniquely appropriate to a purpose and place. Unfortunately, architects are such agile learners that they take this capacity for granted and often miss extraordinary opportunities.

An opportunity is missed simply by confining learning to the project at hand. Architects have historically relied upon the project delivery process for learning. In fact, "most incremental changes in practice involve learning embedded in ongoing projects" (Price 1997). The operative word here is "incremental," with information taking years to accumulate, be connected and interpreted, and eventually used. It's little surprise that, in spite of the amount and type of information to which the entire design team is exposed on every project, the profession is often spoken of as belonging primarily to its most senior members. "Architecture is an old man's profession" is an unfortunate cliché in part because it presumes

Bright Idea

In *The Professional Service Firm 50,* Tom Peters states that he wants everyone in a service firm:

> "To be on a path to personal mastery.

> To be engaged in a calling.

> To be devoted to learning new stuff . . . by hook or by crook . . . every day.

> To eschew complacency like the plague.

> To take enormous pride in an expanding arsenal of skills and knowledge.

> To take the word *research* very seriously."

(Peters 1999)

that personal experience is the only legitimate teacher.

However, it does point to a second missed opportunity: the legacy of wisdom. One of the most daunting, yet critical, challenges for firms is capturing and transferring individual experience and tacit knowledge from one generation to the next. Actually, if staff at all levels realized what they knew, processed it, and made it available to others, the impact on the firm would be transformational. An internal professional development program mandates the conversion of individual experience into integrated knowledge, collaboration, and institutional wisdom.

A third opportunity is missed in the assumption that the architect's professional development is appropriately confined to design and construction matters. The designer's goal is to create the best possible solution in response to the assignment. And the designer will be the first person to explain that the optimum solution demands a thorough investigation of the client and the client's goals. But in the interests of time and economy, and of other projects in the office that demand immediate attention, the architect rarely widens his or her perspective to consider the client's business as a whole. Architects are so focused on channeling expertise and effort into the project that they brush aside any new insights about the client that don't pertain to the immediate problem. Such tunnel vision may expedite projects, but it undermines the architect's leadership potential with many clients.

Richard W. Hobbs, FAIA, in his work as the AIA's Resident Fellow for Marketplace Research, described the architect's knowing/learning activity on projects as leadership, with the architect "absorbing all of the

Key Point
The key is to transform random learning into active knowledge building.

chaos and information and designing a meaningful pattern amid the spatter" (*AIArchitect* March 2001). Hobbs advocates that such "information absorption" should be client-focused and should be composed of both "internal" and "external" knowledge. Internal is "that which is developed by the firm, on an ongoing basis, for each client/project type in which the firm focuses. External knowledge comprises those trends and business strategies that will affect the client and, in turn, the services and the value proposition that the architect contributes toward the client's competitive advantage." So, while the design process does, and should, contribute to the architect's professional expertise and insight, it should also result in a deeper understanding of clients.

All three of these situations—a passive attitude about knowledge building, lost wisdom, and an anecdotal understanding of the client's world—can be easily addressed through a professional development program. Most of the energy in a design firm is channeled into client projects, and the design process can be adjusted to return better insights and information to the firm. Then, projects become not just problems to be solved in the moment; they are learning laboratories in which all team members grow professionally. And the benefit can extend to the rest of the office. Not only should everyone on a design team know more about a client and about practice at the end of a project than at the beginning, but through formal in-house teaching and learning mechanisms, that knowledge can spread throughout the firm.

The key is to transform random learning into active knowledge building. As practitioners know all too well, exposure to information and ideas doesn't

Terms

I deliberately avoid the term "knowledge management," which in the corporate world usually refers to processes for accumulating and sharing data and information. Knowledge building is a much broader experience, which may be supported by "knowledge-management" systems.

Competitive Edge

equal learning. Whether they are wearing headsets, and regardless of the presence or absence of partitions, staff members working at adjoining stations may overhear discussions about other projects; but that does not mean they have absorbed any information that was exchanged within their hearing. On the micro level in design firms, a standard frustration is the reinventing-the-wheel activity, when staff squander precious resources in pursuit of a solution that has just been tested elsewhere and either been perfected or found wanting. On the macro level, a recurring tragedy is the relegation of teaching and learning to ancillary activities, discrete and unrelated to anything else in the office. Learning requires thoughtful consideration, interpretation, and, most important, *sharing*. Investigation, discussion, and debate are already mundane elements of practice. Raising participants' consciousness of these activities is a first step in enhancing their professional development.

Business Excellence

From a simple business perspective, a continuing education program enhances the firm's performance. For one thing, a firm that invests in the professional development of its staff also addresses an age-old challenge for any service firm: staff attrition. In his book, *Intellectual Capital: The New Wealth of Organizations* (1999), Thomas Stewart considers the "fundamental conundrum of human capital: People can be rented, but not owned." He points out that, "Valuable, hard-to-replace knowledge, the key to competitive advantage, is forged in communities of practice, but they and the human capital they create are no respecters of shareholder value." People who

Key Point

A professional development program can and should be designed to sustain and replenish the firm's resources.

have learned skills and grown professionally in one firm may very well decide to move on, taking their insights with them. Rather than rush to protect experienced professionals, or to drag their heels on knowledge building among staff, firms cautious about staff transience should run toward professional development. As Stewart points out, "A vibrant learning community socializes human capital, which gives the company a stake in it." A custom of shared knowledge reduces the impact of any one person's departure.

And people are less likely to want to leave a firm that attends to their professional development. Research indicates that employees value training and related programs that help them do their jobs better. Architecture firms increasingly credit in-house professional development programs with improvements in profitability, as well as in quality control. Marketing is also enhanced, both directly, through improved skills, and indirectly, through a closer connection to clients. Some firms that have implemented professional development programs are finding that not only are their clients impressed by commitment to lifelong learning, they want to share in it. Clients are asking to sit in on sessions, as both teachers and learners, and they are seeking the advice of their architects on setting up programs inside their own real estate and design groups. Competitive edge doesn't get much sharper.

Since 1998, the AIA's Continuing Education System has conducted half a dozen Leadership Summits on professional development. Part of each summit is a brainstorming session during which participants address the misconception that continuing education drains resources. During one typical session in

Point Clear, Alabama, representatives of 13 design firms from across the United States identified some of the ways that a proprietary program enhances a firm's viability. Roughly condensed and translated, their ideas seem to fall within six business areas: strategic effectiveness, financial performance, leadership, quality, marketing, and staffing.

The 50 enhancements shown in the box on the next page can be provided by an internal program.

A professional development program can and should be designed to sustain and replenish the firm's resources.

Innovation

Architectural practice is about innovation and change, each contributing to the other. The creativity inherent in design means that people consider alternatives, put ideas together in a new way, and create change. High standards for performance and service, and the daily accumulation and application of experience, also feed innovation and encourage change. Outside the firm, shifting social/political/economic patterns, sophisticated and demanding clients, new and evolving markets, technology, competitors, and other factors over which the firm has little control, demand new approaches. Usually, firms experience change subtly, but most designers can recall transformations that were fast, conspicuous, and sometimes painful.

Since innovation is natural to a design firm, and change is inevitable, firms must at the very least be alert to events that may affect them in the future, be receptive to possible outcomes, and be able to adjust quickly. At best, firms can actively invoke staff to be

Key Point

An innovation-friendly firm has a better chance at charting its own course and thriving, rather than merely adapting.

50 Enhancements Provided by an Internal Program

To Strategic Effectiveness

Improve reaction to industry trends.

Increase project type expertise.

Stimulate creative environment.

Support firm's long-range goals.

Stimulate staff.

Increase scope of services.

Clarify market niches.

To Leadership

Increase visionary power.

Improve ability to promote from within.

Improve skills and services.

Increase staff responsibility.

Improve management skills.

Improve business literacy.

To the Firm's Financial Performance

Focus management on efficiency.

Identify most profitable services.

Identify profit leaks.

Focus resources.

Weave learning into billable activity.

Reduce liability.

Increase productivity.

Identify unprofitable processes.

Reduce external training costs.

Improve risk management.

Increase capacity.

Address scheduling issues.

To Quality

Integrate learning into project delivery.

Reduce errors and omissions.

Refine design.

Identify lessons learned on projects.

Provide training.

Enhance capability for quality projects.

To Marketing

Improve marketing win rate.

Educate clients.

Identify client needs.

Provide new market skills.

Improve client satisfaction.

Turn satisfied clients into repeat work.

Reduce marketing expense.

Understand client services.

Be promoted as a marketing asset.

To Staffing

Improve staff retention.

Improve quality of staff.

Enhance recruiting.

Create positive work environment.

Improve morale.

Improve team development.

Address employee concerns/goals.

Unite technical and support staff.

Offer professional growth.

inquisitive, to review and question what they are doing, to test new things, and to transfer their findings into practice. An innovation-friendly firm has a better chance at charting its own course and thriving, rather than merely adapting.

From the time that it is instituted, an internal professional development program enhances a firm's capability to innovate and lead, both attitudinally and functionally. In terms of attitude, a program:

- ▶ Turns a spotlight on information and experience.

- ▶ Raises people's consciousness about knowledge and learning.

- ▶ Emboldens people to interpret what they observe and experience.

- ▶ Spurs them to try different things, differently.

Knowledge sharing whets the appetite for fresh ideas and dulls the fear of change. Learning abets learning.

In organizational terms, a firm's proprietary continuing education program serves as a framework for facilitating innovation. It is a system within which trends are researched and people develop skills and knowledge that will propel the firm toward its desired future. Two of the most promising areas to be studied in any firm are its client base and the markets those clients represent. Learning from and about clients for the benefit of projects is part of the design process. Enlarging the activity so that the firm is learning from and about clients for the benefit of clients paves the way for innovations that add a new dimension to client service. Design firms can institute learning practices that help them to escalate their understanding of their clients' universe: the place where clients live and the environment in which clients operate. Architects can more clearly comprehend their clients' dreams and long-range plans, so that design services, processes, and solutions can pave a smoother road to reaching them. Research and development activities are as critical to a design firm's future as they are to the life of a biotech start-up or a hopeful software developer.

In addition to spurring innovation, the professional development system can serve as a mechanism for expediting change. For example, not only could a firm anticipating ownership transition provide management workshops, it could beef up training in budgets and schedules for junior staff members who will have to take on more responsibility. It could revise project roles so that potential new principals could work on their coaching and mentoring skills. It could develop initiatives on marketing and networking to address experience gaps created when transitioning principals leave.

Similarly, a firm that has decided that it needs to deepen its value to an existing market can tap into its in-house professional development system. The firm could, for example, provide presentations about the market, adjust its ongoing project manager development program to reflect evolving service needs of the client base, establish collaborative training and mentoring ventures with consultants who specialize in the market, and import workshops provided by manufacturers of materials and products preferred by the market.

Design firms accommodate change as a matter of course. An internal professional development program positions a firm to do three things: plan how it will change and innovate; pursue, rather than accommodate, change; and stimulate the energy and creativity that sparks innovation.

Reinforcing Culture

The core of a design firm's individuality is its culture, and every firm demonstrates its distinct cultural attributes, whether it means to or not. Outsiders, as well as insiders, experience the culture, even as they struggle to describe it. Visceral and amorphous, a firm's culture encompasses its history and accomplishments, its leaders' ambitions and goals, its definition of and criteria for excellence, its attitude about clients and staff, its traditions and lore, its mood and energy, and its balance between art and business, among other things. Vague though culture may be, in the marketplace for clients and staff, cultural match is a criterion for selection and a yardstick for performance.

Key Point

In the marketplace for clients and staff, cultural match is a criterion for selection and a yardstick for performance.

For design firms, two of the most distinct, and distinguishable, cultural aspects are *values* and *personality*.

Values

Values are the deep motivations and core beliefs that consistently drive important decisions and shape the firm's design and business priorities. When Arie de Geus describes characteristics that "living" corporations are likely to demonstrate, most of his description alludes to values. In his vision, the long-lived company exists to thrive, and one of its core values is to be the best it can be. Its members share common values. The connection between corporate values and personal values is so close that people's personal goals are reached with the company's whole-hearted support. The skills of employees are valued; employ-

Key Point

Values shape firms.

ees are trusted, and trusting. Members of the company are skilled in ways that the company appreciates (de Geus 1997).

Furthermore, according to de Geus, the company is receptive to the outside world, and leaders are mindful of generations to come. The company is fiscally responsible; once it is secure, its capital assets and economic activity are used to develop its potential. When it is threatened, the living company will try to change the nature of its economic activity before it lets its people go. The living company is a learning organism, and it acts on the basis of a learning process (ibid).

Design firms hold core values, too. Values shape firms as much as, if not more than, they affect the businesses cited in De Geus's work. Three powerful value indicators in a design firm are *decision making, information sharing,* and *authority.* People infer values in how decisions are made on projects and on general business questions: Do the most senior people make all decisions, or are conclusions drawn through consensus? What, and how, information is shared in the firm also reflects the firm's values. How generous are firm leaders in communicating with people about project and business matters? Does the firm convey detailed information through formal presentations and reports? Or incrementally, on a need-to-know basis? Or casually through the office grapevine? Authority and autonomy reflect values of importance to people at every level in a firm. To what degree is responsibility delegated, and to whom? What is the correlation between responsibility and autonomy?

Classifying design firm values has been the purpose of significant research conducted in the past 20 years. Several theories have been constructed around a firm's approach to client service. In the 1980s, The Coxe Group, management consultants to design firms, and David Maister, their peer for attorneys, indicated that firms generally manifest core values through two things: (1) a tendency to operate either as a "practice-centered business" or as a "business-centered practice," and (2) a technological approach to projects that addresses client needs primarily through strong ideas, or strong service, or strong delivery (Coxe, et al. 1986).

Since then, two other consulting firms have devoted considerable effort to investigating the driving forces within design firms. The SPARKS Center for Strategic Planning seems to agree with The Coxe Group that a firm's essential purpose is revealed through the means it uses to contribute value to its client base, but SPARKS has identified six archetypes (the Einstein, Niche Player, Market Partner, Community Leader, Orchestrator, Builder) each of which reflects a distinct business focus (Flynn-Heapes 2000). Alternatively the Advanced Management Institute (AMI) posits an "ecology" of design firms. In this thesis, as in the others, a firm's business should reflect the firm's preferred clients and the clients' preferred product; however, the AMI model also incorporates the firm's preferred project team organization into the equation (Kyle V. Daly and Susan L. Harris 2001).

These models, and most others that have been proposed for the design professions, seem to suggest that the kinds of clients to whom one chooses to devote one's practice, and the techniques one chooses to employ in order to provide the best possible service, together represent a clear manifestation of a design firm's values. In any case, whether one thinks of values in such terms as those proposed by experienced design firm consultants or as those observed by business visionaries like de Geus, core values shape organizations. People inside a design firm, and people outside the firm, observe and experience those values. Compelling values attract clients and staff.

Personality

A second powerful aspect of culture for design firms is character, or "personality." Personality is less researched and more difficult to identify than values, but it is often as compelling, even for clients.

Client satisfaction surveys unearth aspects of a firm's personality. Surveys also provide evidence of the power of personality. In satisfaction assessments, clients typically comment as much on the apparent attitudes of design firm personnel as they do on the service itself, and as much on the mood and tone of the design process as on the process itself.

For example, in speaking about a Chicago firm that had completed a large wellness center for a community healthcare provider, the client homed in on the architect's inclusive leadership style, saying, "The architectural firm served as very proactive team leaders. They were able to feed on, and feed, all the members of the team in dealing with complex issues" (Blackridge, Ltd. 1999). In a different survey, an oil company's facilities director was impressed by the atmosphere permeating a Texas firm, saying, "When you walk into that office, people obviously feel open, and can express their opinions freely. You see people helping each other; there's a sense of pride and team." Other clients of the firm echoed this

Tip

One way to get a sense of your firm's personality as your clients experience it is to ask all of them a few qualitative questions. Accumulate their answers over a month or two, and then look for patterns. You could ask:

► What was your initial impression of our firm you when you first encountered us? Has your impression changed?

► If someone asked you to describe the personality or mood of our firm, what would you answer?

observation (ibid), suggesting that a collaborative style is highly valued, and practiced, inside this particular office—and that clients enjoy the synergy.

Clients frequently use this kind of language to describe the personality of "their" architecture firm as they experience it through project engagement.

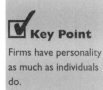

Insider: Mark Tortorich, FAIA. Personality of a Design Firm

In 1999, while I was researching client perceptions about a West Coast architecture firm, I spoke with Mark Tortorich, FAIA, who at that time was a GSA project executive with the Design Excellence Program. I tested Blackridge's theory about the power of design firm "personality" with him, and found he had clearly been thinking along the same lines. Tortorich now consults with private and public institutions as a principal of URS, and he continues his relationship with the GSA as a private sector Design Excellence peer advisor. Here, he shares some of his thoughts.

After evaluating hundreds of architecture firms for public and private commissions, I have come to realize that firms have a personality as much as individuals do. Synonymous with office culture, personality encompasses core characteristics of the firm that transcend initial impressions. Prospective clients need to assess these characteristics and evaluate what works for them on a particular project. Some clients are looking for their architect to be a clone, a compatible yet distinct individual, a dreamer, or an agitator.

What is the value of personality to a client? Personality defines how the architectural practice investigates the problem, how it searches for solutions, and how it finally settles on a plan of action. Since each site, program, and client is a unique circumstance, personality provides continuity throughout the portfolio. Marketing materials, office décor, design philosophy, and even the office dress code reveal a firm's personality to prospective clients.

An identifiable personality allows a prospective client to evaluate the important issues for making architecture, and opens the door to a productive relationship. However, if not properly assessed during the selection phase, a client may become frustrated with the architect's personality during the course of the project. Simply relying on a firm's size or past experience will not reveal anything about the culture of the office. From my experience, clients must take time to understand the firm's character by interviewing essential personnel, talking to former clients, visiting past projects, and observing the studio environment.

Through the course of a project, I witness the firm through the eyes of the designer, technician, administrator, accountant, and principal, providing a broader perspective of the firm's true character. Sometimes this experience reinforces my initial impressions and forges a lasting bond that results in repeat business. I find myself returning to the firm in the same way I seek out old friends.

A change in ownership or design leadership can dramatically alter a firm's personality and therefore test the bonds built through previous experiences. For example, the rapid growth of a boutique firm into a significant practice: The firm grows so quickly that it loses the personal touch of the founder and design principal. Issues take longer to resolve, and include intermediaries. Instead of providing opportunities for an emerging talent, I am stuck with a time-challenged celebrity. Firm acquisitions and mergers create a particular challenge. In rare cases, these acquisitions suppress the tangible and appealingly quirky characteristics of an entrepreneurial practice. More frequently, however, these acquisitions pump new life into a firm by providing innovative leadership and the capital to update facilities and equipment.

Professional journals and institutions reinforce the image of architects as solitary masters by awarding individuals, not teams or firms, with honors and recognition. This supplies the media with the personalities they desperately need to make the connection between architect and architecture. Firms need to recognize this reality, and pay attention to their own personality as they talk to clients about making architecture (Tortorich 2002).

Bolstering Culture through Professional Development

Values and personality are real to clients and to staff. Because they distinguish firms from one another, values and personality are fundamental ingredients of competitive edge. And they should not be taken for granted.

In a sole proprietorship or a new firm, personality and values are easy to identify; they naturally pervade the firm, because they are the owner's. The entrepreneur looks for people whose personalities and values are compatible with hers or his. A sense of mutual understanding often permeates the office. For many professionals, working in such an environment is one of the most satisfying times in professional practice, even when one isn't that entrepreneur.

However, as a firm matures, as more key staff members contribute to the shaping of the firm, and especially as the firm grows, its values evolve and its personality changes. Its culture becomes richer and more complex. This evolution is as healthy as it is natural. But along the way, such things as inadequate communications, shifting client base and expanded services, additions of personnel in newly created roles, and incorrect assumptions about mutual goals can cause the universally sensed culture to dissipate and to become confused and less compelling.

At such times, a firm's leaders often reconnect among themselves and with the firm through a long-range planning initiative, articulating their mission, clarifying values, and charting new goals. Personality, even if it is not addressed directly, is also typically clearer. Increasingly, such planning efforts include a learning program for the firm to help rally staff and jump-start their plan. In fact, at any given point in time, professional development can be an engine for either sustaining the firm's vision and culture or for changing them.

A client's sense of a design firm's culture is a powerful factor in her or his decision to retain or recommend the firm in the future. Similarly, staff are stimulated by the firm's character. Typically, a reliable sample of any firm's clients and staff repeats themes in discussing the firm's strengths or weaknesses, and many of those themes are cultural in nature. The themes most often cited should reflect the firm's most cherished values and personality traits. A thoughtfully designed internal professional development program articulates those values and personality, applies them to daily practice, and conveys them clearly to the firm's constituencies.

Improving Competitive Edge: The Purpose of This Book

A healthy culture, ability to innovate, business excellence, and, of course, active knowledge building enrich professional practice and distinguish firms from each other. The purpose of this book is to help design firms and individual professionals to improve their competitive position in the marketplace by planning and implementing their own proprietary professional development programs. To that end, this book focuses on continuing professional development rather than on training. It is about deepening and broadening whole expertise over time, rather than moving through the initial stages of professional skill building and awareness.

Organization of the Book

The book is organized chronologically in the order that one would, if one were so well organized and prescient, address professional development. I begin with educational strategy, then move into assessment, planning, and program design. Next you will find descriptions of each of three practice-oriented learning methods—classroom courses, lessons-learned activities, and mentoring—and suggestions for implementation. The final chapters discuss processes for evaluating your educational initiatives and for using that information to improve performance. Finally, in the Appendix of the book, I offer learning objectives. For each chapter I have suggested learn-

Note

Intern development and career planning for people just entering the profession are not addressed in these pages, simply because there wasn't time to do justice to the full range of topics. I will only say that design firms often report that their intern development programs benefit substantially as lifelong learning programs are instituted for experienced staff, and I hope that people new to the profession will be intrigued by the prospect of a lifetime of learning.

ing objectives and ancillary activities that can themselves comprise a learning module. You can easily adapt the learning objectives to reflect your specific goals and adjust the activities similarly.

Mavericks and Sole Proprietors

You will also note that most chapters end with a section titled "Mavericks and Sole Proprietors" (with a tip of the hat to Robert Douglass, FAIA, and his doctor of design thesis, "Maverick Architects: Success in Non-traditional Careers," Harvard University, 1994). Design professionals are not all members of large, or even midsized, architecture firms. Many prefer to practice independently, or to serve as architecture experts in engineering or construction firms, or to sit in the client role as facilities managers or campus architects. Some are photographers, writers, teachers, critics, lawyers, financial advisors, and public servants. Without the resources, support, or momentum of an organization, the maverick must be more alert, agile, and forward-looking.

One forward-looking maverick is Richard Hobbs, to whom I alluded earlier in this chapter. Competitive edge is much on his mind, too.

Insider Richard W. Hobbs, FAIA: The Three-legged Stool

Richard Hobbs, FAIA, is president of Strategy Design, Inc., consultants to the design community in the areas of vision and strategy. Having served as AIA vice president for Professional Practice and as AIA Resident Fellow in Marketplace Research, Hobbs studies and writes extensively about the architecture of practice. His "three-legged stool" metaphor suggests how firms can use learning as a support for the changes that keep a practice healthy and client-focused.

In an economy and business world ruled by ideas, knowledge, and innovation, the only form of sustainable leadership is that which puts a premium on well-designed

---

and implemented strategy. Many of us are wondering today how to define a long-term strategy in an economy that moves at the speed of sound, or even as fast as the Internet.

Leaders in the design profession are recognizing that the marketplace in which they practice is ever changing. Leaders are seeing an increasing awareness of the value they provide to their clients. Leaders recognize that when the skill sets—the knowledge—is properly integrated, it enables innovation, which, in turn, produces client satisfaction and competitive advantage for the firm.

The key to a well-defined and implemented business strategy, in a knowledge-driven world in which reinvention is a constant, is lifelong learning.

We have moved past talking about *whether* to reinvent our firms within the profession; we are in the *how*, the mechanics of carrying it out. The challenge is "*How* can a firm transform an existing culture into a new culture and fulfill its vision?"

This transformation, this reinvention can be seen as supported by a three-legged stool. The seat of the stool is the reinvention of the practice entity; the legs are made up of *leadership, businesses strategy*, and *knowledge management*.

Leadership is about vision, strategy, and preparing organizations for change. Change within the organization is necessary to add greater value in one's particular marketplace. Management, in turn, is about coping with the complexity within the change.

Any long-term *business strategy* starts with focus, meaning the definition of the business one is really in, and the value, the differentiation, provided within the market(s) in which one is contributing value to the client.

Once a business strategy is developed, a *knowledge management* system is needed to support the strategy. How does one define, develop, and deliver tacit and explicit knowledge? How does one define design and organizational knowledge? How does one integrate subjects, issues, and experiences that add to the knowledge that can be leveraged to provide greater value within the client's marketplace?

This is professional development, a lifetime learning commitment by the profession and the professional entity.

Leaders, understanding the broad opportunities, create, communicate, and empower others to act on the vision. The leadership vision, with a business strategy, sets the stage for knowledge management systems. An integrated knowledge-sharing process provides the maximum focus and maximum return on investment.

The stool needs all three legs. Take a leg out and the stool cannot stay upright. Maintain all three and there is a support from which firms can move into their preferred future of providing knowledge and value to clients and communities, within and beyond the built environment.

Learning is a survival skill, and having a map for knowledge building can be crucial to the maverick's career path. In a sense, all design professionals are mavericks or sole practitioners. Competitive edge and professional development concepts apply to individuals, as well as to organizations.

Strategy

2

Chapter 1 presented four aspects of competitive edge that distinguish design firms from each other in the eyes of people outside and inside the firm. Three of the competitive advantages—business excellence, the ability to innovate, and a healthy culture—can and should be woven into the firm's professional development program. The fourth, knowledge building, is the professional development program.

Knowing things and building knowledge are very different from each other. To become a competitive advantage, knowledge building must be deliberately conceived and thoughtfully designed. As a famous Cheshire cat once suggested, if the little girl in question hadn't a destination in mind, then she might as well choose any old path along the way. Similarly, although knowing things is helpful now and again, knowledge building can lead the firm somewhere.

Strategic Principles

Purposeful knowledge building sharpens a firm's competitive edge. And purposeful knowledge building requires a deliberate strategic approach. The firm must identify its professional development goals and then build a means for reaching them. Guiding the process is a good design that reflects these three strategic principles:

> A firm's knowledge-building activity should include all five elements of a professional development program.

> Professional development should support the firm's business vision.

> Professional development should generate a learning dynamic in which the knowledge of the firm, its staff, and its clients are mustered for the benefit of the firm, its staff, and its clients.

First Principle: Include All Five Elements

As shown in Figure 2.1, the five basic elements of a good internal professional development program are:

1. An educational strategy
2. A process for knowledge assessment
3. The design of an overall program for learning and of individual initiatives
4. Implementation of the program and a system to support it
5. A process for the evaluation and improvement of the learning program

Ideally, a firm would embark on a proprietary learning enterprise by addressing the first element: carefully defined goals and a strategy for building knowledge with the whole-hearted support of the owners of the firm. After those were in place, the firm would analyze its current situation and plan the ways in which professional development will move the firm toward achievement of its goals. Educational programs would then be designed and implemented to respond to the plan. And, finally, at

Figure 2.1 Basic elements of a good internal professional development program. © 2002 Blackridge, Ltd.

predetermined checkpoints, the program's success would be evaluated and remedial actions taken to keep it on track.

Such chronological progress has been experienced by some very organized firms, I'm sure. But a more realistic way to think about these five activities is as elements, rather than steps, and to respect the way in which most firms actually embark on learning programs.

Typically, design firms start at elements 3 and 4 by developing a few workshops or by lining up a number of manufacturers to deliver lunch and lectures at regular intervals. Starting here is the easiest jump-start to a program. The firm builds the workshops into a series, then starts adding more events. Next the firm does a little of number 5 by evaluating the workshops and asking staff what kinds of new programs they'd like to see. Later, someone briefly steps back and takes an overall view of the enterprise (1) to compare subject matter with the firm's long-range goals. Finally, having looked ahead at the goals and behind at the wandering footprints, the firm arrives at number 2, rightly determining that assessing needs and designing learning activities expressly to address them will boost the program's effectiveness and efficiency.

Such an organic approach to learning programs can be very effective. In fact, many mature programs embrace serendipity. Firms that have had training programs in place for years, such as HOK and Gensler, are famous for encouraging grassroots learning and research initiatives. For every FreemanWhite that began with a powerful leadership mandate and a strategic professional development plan, there is a Rosser International or a Lukemire Partnership where a spark in the mind of one or two staff members kindles quietly as a cluster of learning events before catching throughout the firm. Quality programs ignite from the smallest glimmer. Firms need to start where they are and understand that shaping a solid program is likely to take 18 to 24 months.

Regardless of where a firm starts, and in what order the elements are addressed, the goal is for *strategy, assessment, design, implementation*, and *evaluation and improvement* to form a cyclical process through which knowledge-building is perpetually enriched.

Second Principle: Support the Firm's Vision

Leadership strategy is essential to the success of a professional development program, because the firm's professional development strategy must be conceived and grown out of the firm's overall vision and business plan.

Most firms have a vision or a long-range plan for their future. Articulated or merely understood, the

Tip

Excellent professional development programs share five common attributes:

▶ *Deliberation.* The learning program is thoughtfully developed.

▶ *Focus on learning.* Success is measured by the degree to which people actually learn.

▶ *Objectivity.* Needs and performance are measured in a variety of ways.

▶ *Processes.* Professional development is expedited through user-friendly systems and processes.

▶ *Continuous improvement.* Review and evaluation procedures result in enhancements at least yearly.

vision includes the goals a firm sets, the kind of clients and projects it wishes to pursue, the value it will contribute to clients, and the type of staff it intends to recruit and develop. More and more firms are choosing to verbalize and publish their vision; to identify their mission, core values, and practice goals; and to draft a long-range plan for making their vision real.

The firm's vision and plan determine the three significant parties that will comprise the firm's activity: the firm itself, its staff, and its clients. The firm is an entity that includes portfolio, history, systems, and a cadre of consultant relationships, as well as the culture, values, and personality discussed in Chapter 1. The staff includes the people whose talents, knowledge, and experience reside in the firm at any given moment. Clients are the organizations and individuals that retain the firm, as well as the public at large who are affected by completed spaces and places.

Through day-to-day practice, the three parties subtly reshape the firm's long-range plan and often the vision. An effective professional development program anticipates this constant refreshment of vision and plan, and in fact stimulates the refinement of both.

Third Principle: Generate a Learning Dynamic

The voluble nature of practice requires that the firm's learning program be dynamic and that learning be rooted at the place where the firm, its clients, and its staff intersect (see Figure 2.2).

An effective learning strategy ensures that knowledge within the firm *is fed from* the:

> ➤ Firm's growing portfolio, experience, and consultant relationships

Tip

In the absence of an updated long-range plan, particularly when the current press of work diverts leadership's attention from vision to urgent matters, professional development proponents might try assuming that the firm's long-range goal is to be exactly what it is today, only more so. Proceeding on that basis is likely to highlight the firm's prevailing direction and inspire decision making, either to sprint along the current path or to change direction.

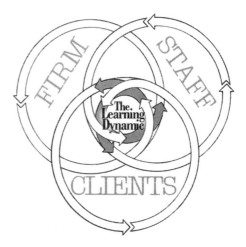

Figure 2.2 The Learning Dynamic. © 2002 Blackridge, Ltd.

- Ever-changing skills and experience of its staff
- Changing needs and expertise of its clients

An effective learning strategy also ensures that knowledge accumulating within the firm *feeds* the:

- Firm's expertise and potential
- Professional development of staff
- Firm's understanding of, and contribution to, its clients

Daily practice assails people with ideas, data, insights, experiences, and information orts, primarily around the urgent needs of clients and teams. A strategic approach to knowledge building requires that people think about capturing learning opportunities, embrace formal skills training, test ideas, conduct research, and share insights in a way that moves the firm toward its long-term goals.

To reap the benefits of a learning dynamic, information and perceptions should flow from projects and clients into the firm, where they are synthesized by staff members in light of their own and the firm's experience, and incorporated into the firm's body of knowledge. The firm and the staff gain new insights. The knowledge itself flows back in a new and enriched form through many projects, the better to serve clients and the public at large. Positioned at the point where knowledge converges inside a firm, the dynamic learning program should advance the firm's long-range plan.

FreemanWhite: Connecting Business and Educational Plans

FreemanWhite, Inc. has an award-winning continuing education program that reflects the incorporation of all three strategic design principles: the five basic elements of a good program, support of the firm's business vision, and use of the learning dynamic. Recipient of the American Institute of Architects Continuing Education System (AIA/CES) 2001 large firm Award for Excellence, the program is clearly linked to the firm's 1992 strategic plan. During a comprehensive planning process that year, FreemanWhite's senior management decided to take the firm in a new direction based on a "narrow and deep" vision that would limit the types of clients the firm served, but expand the services offered to those clients. In their strategic vision, the firm's leaders agreed to add nontraditional consulting services to their architectural expertise and to diversify and expand staff capabilities. FreemanWhite's vision encompassed six rallying ideas:

Key Point

Keeping in mind the concepts presented in Chapter 1, we can look at the way FreemanWhite hones competitive edge through a learning program that both reinforces the organization's culture and facilitates the achievement of new corporate goals.

1. **Idea-Based Professional Services Firm**
   ▶ Core Business: Problem-solving/Design/ Creativity/Results

2. **Experts in Three Prime Markets**
   - ➤ Health Care
   - ➤ Government
   - ➤ Senior Living
3. **Experts in Three Areas of Service**
   - ➤ Strategy/Market forecasting/Organizational Change
   - ➤ Operational Analysis
   - ➤ Facility Planning and Design
4. **Hire "the Best and the Brightest"**
   - ➤ Develop Leadership
   - ➤ Continuing Professional Development
5. **Deliver "The FreemanWhite Experience"**
   - ➤ Focus on Our Client's Business Success
6. **Leave a Legacy**

The vision led to six goals, each of which had ramifications for practice and client service. Of particular note is the fact that FreemanWhite's goals addressed the way that the firm intended to contribute value to clients through design, service, project delivery, and research. By the "measurable results" goal, the leadership team meant that the firm was to accumulate data that would quantify the benefit clients received from the firm's services. The goals:

"The FreemanWhite Experience"
Live and breathe it.

Innovative Solutions
Do great work!

Measurable Results
Document the value we create!

Strengthen Our Credibility

One of a select few!

Work Smart

Efficiency–Quality–Speed to Market.

Grow Smart

Maintain our narrow and deep focus!

When a firm so specifically identifies the ways in which it intends to enhance clients' experience, it aims the firm toward professional development. And, in fact, FreemanWhite did so, literally. Each goal points directly to a learning initiative, starting with "The FreemanWhite Experience," leading to a cultural rudiment, "Learning is respected," and ending with the business point that managed growth would be supported by the opportunities that learning creates (see Figure 2.3).

The six continuing education initiatives, supplemented with the following five specific educational goals (see Figure 2.4), formed the core of Freeman-White's first strategic educational plan:

Today, FreemanWhite ensures that its educational plan keeps pace with its broader vision and culture. Following senior management's annual long-term planning sessions, learning initiatives have been reviewed, in terms of new business goals, and adjusted accordingly. In terms of culture, furthering "The FreemanWhite Way" continues to be a stated goal. Manifestations of "The FreemanWhite Way" are built into many course offerings. And the professional development program features a number of "culture courses" on such topics as the firm's history and the firm's distinct approach to leadership.

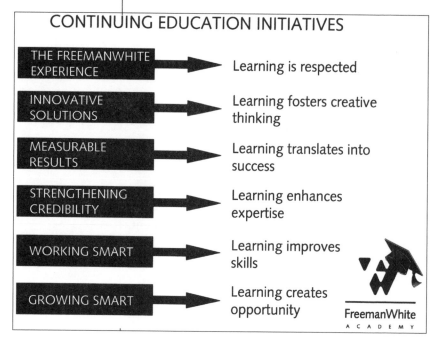

Figure 2.3 FreemanWhite's continuing education initiatives.

Moving from Strategic Principles to Strategic Plan

A strategic plan for professional development is a handy resource for the people who are responsible for developing and monitoring the learning venture. Whether in verbal or graphic format or a combination of both, similar to FreemanWhite's, the plan presents the rationale behind the proprietary program, expressly in terms of the knowledge and skills needed for the firm to attain its practice mission. The plan should be revised annually and supported by yearly implementation plans (see Figure 2.5). Perhaps the greatest value of a regular professional development planning process is that it contributes substantially to the integrity of the firm's vision. A plan for know-

FreemanWhite
A C A D E M Y

EDUCATION GOALS

To provide continuous learning throughout the employee's career
- From Orientation through Career Development
- Resting on The FreemanWhite Academy

To provide employees with the knowledge and skills to meet individual job performance expectations and professional continuing education requirements
- Job-specific curriculum in "The FreemanWhite Way"
- Maintain licenses and professional memberships

To provide knowledge interconnectivity across
- The Firm's Strategic Goals, Systems & Culture
- The Three Markets: Healthcare, Government & Senior Living
- The Service Disciplines: Strategy, Operational Analysis & Design

To provide flexibility in subject matter and delivery methods
- Freedom of self–directed stipend and enrichment classes with structure of corporate–directed methods and core classes

To strengthen the profession by offering continuing education courses to fellow practitioners
- Fostering professional fellowship and advancement of the profession

Figure 2.4 FreemanWhite's educational goals.

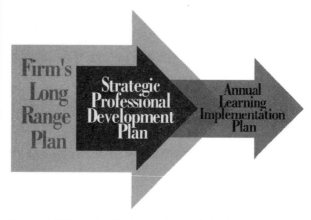

Figure 2.5 Strategic plan for professional development.

ledge building prepares staff for the firm's future and enables a firm's vision to be realized.

The Plan: Content

The learning plan is a succinct outline of key points about the firm's process for continuing the professional growth of staff members. The plan is not a manual; it should not describe in detail the firm's professional development processes. Rather, it should touch on all five elements (strategy, assessment, design, implementation, evaluation and improvement) and identify the:

1. Connection between the firm's long-range plan and its professional development goals.

2. Process by which the firm's leadership will set the overall educational direction and review progress.

3. Means through which learning needs will be assessed.

4. Process for developing the overall professional development program.

5. Approach to investing in, and benefiting from, the learning program.

6. System for the design and implementation of professional development initiatives.

7. Process for evaluating and improving the professional development program.

1. Connecting Long-Range Plan and Professional Development Goals

Because a firm invests in knowledge building for the sake of organizational vitality and viability, the professional development plan typically begins with three items: a summary of the firm's long-term mission, a summary of the firm's learning goals and their relationship to the long-range plan, and a brief explanation of the process through which the learning plan is correlated to the firm's long-range plan.

Connecting firm goals and professional development goals is essential. For example, Firm ABC may intend over the next five years to focus on the design of public schools, to serve clients in regions beyond its current practice, and to empower its project managers with greater project and marketing responsibility. In contrast, Firm XYZ plans to design public schools, libraries, town halls, and community centers as part of its focus on serving regional municipalities. Even though both firms will design public schools, their plans for learning will be very dissimilar, because the building type is just one aspect of the firm's long-range plan.

2. Involving the Firm's Leadership

Having linked the educational goals firmly to the firm's business strategy, the professional development plan identifies the process through which the

Tip

While considering professional development goals, recall the ideas of Arie de Geus presented in Chapter 1. An architecture firm that aspires to long life could think about using learning programs to imbue itself with "living" capabilities, such as "the ability to learn and adapt," "the ability to build a community and persona for itself," "the ability to build constructive relationships with other entities, within and outside itself," and "the ability to govern its own growth" (de Geus, 1997).

firm's principals and owners will provide strategic perspective to the professional development planning process, set direction for the program, and review progress.

The plan should state both the forum and the form for senior review. The professional development plan might be an agenda item at annual retreats for principals; it might be addressed at monthly management meetings; or it might be reviewed in some other regularly scheduled forum. In terms of role, some firms expect their principals to approve a plan and budget developed by others. Principals might set all or some strategic educational goals. Firm leaders might be expected to participate in the program as learners or teachers. Their involvement might include the selection of a professional development champion from among their own ranks. Whatever the nature of principal involvement, the integrity and quality of a firm's program are reflected in part by the consistency of principal involvement.

3. Assessing Needs and Opportunities

The plan also must address the rationale for determining subject matter. It will suggest sources and activities that will be used to pinpoint skills and information that are missing in the firm, and to indicate opportunities for importing new skills, information, and aptitudes into the firm.

The firm might decide to look outside, to consultants or periodicals, for annual market and design trends. It could perform a benchmark client satisfaction survey to be conducted again in three years' time. Many firms involve staff in employee surveys. Focus groups, perhaps of department managers, represent another common approach to assessment.

Some firms look at criteria for performance reviews and promotions as a basis for determining the areas that professional development should address. Other indicators might be found in change orders, quality control issues, insurance rates, and the like.

Gathering information from several sources is likely to provide more reliable information. One economical approach might be to begin with one assessment process and then add new processes, as annual results or a revised long-range plan seem to dictate. In any case, the plan should state how instruments or data will be used to determine needs and opportunities.

4. Establishing a Program

Another key item of the plan is a description of the process the firm uses to design the learning program. Typically, firms rely on one leader, or champion, supported by a committee process. Under the champion's direction, a dedicated standing committee creates the professional development plan and monitors its implementation. Ad hoc task forces convene for specific purposes, such as assessing needs, researching specific learning options, identifying costs, or outlining a mentoring process.

The champion may be a principal, human resources director, in-house "dean," quality control leader, or any staff member with a passion for learning, communication skills, and the ability to listen effectively to senior and junior staff. Composition of the standing committee is as important as identification of the champion. The decisions made about "involving the firm's leadership" (number 2) will determine the degree to which principals participate on the committee. The committee is further helped

Tip

The most current resource for architects interested in continuing education is the American Institute of Architects' Continuing Education System. Organizations that are AIA/CES registered providers of educational programs receive a copy of the *CES Provider Manual*, which is updated and published online annually.

when members collectively have expertise in such matters as:

Training	Familiar with the opportunities, techniques, and limitations of professional development.
IDP	Understands the requirements of the National Certification and Architectural Registration Board's (NCARB) Intern Development Program.
Firm leadership	Provides a big-picture perspective on professional practice.
Human resources	Knowledgeable about recruiting and retaining staff; well versed in the firm's performance review criteria and process.
Quality control	Expert in design, documentation, and matters related to health, safety, and welfare.
IT	Alert to administrative applications, as well as project-related functions, of information technology.
Marketing	Understands market and client trends.

Missing expertise can be provided through professional development consultants, colleagues from other firms, the American Institute of Architects, an AIA chapter, or by committee members willing to do some homework.

To improve communications and commitment, professional development committees often reflect the firm's organizational structure, with representatives from all departments, studios, and/or offices. But structure and process must arise from the firm's actual investment in knowledge building. Some firms may deliberately choose to start small by outlining a test program for one studio or office, and then, after some demonstrated success, to modify the process for broader application. The professional development plan would lay out such a graduated approach, and committee composition would adjust accordingly. In fact, rotating membership on the committee may be the best way to ensure energy, fresh ideas, and ever-broadening support for professional development.

The plan should summarize the committee's composition, responsibilities, reporting structure, and method of operation.

5. *Determining Investment and Return*

The plan notes the process for identifying and establishing the nature and degree of the firm's investment in professional development. In some firms, the process rests on the professional development standing committee, which itself prepares conceptual budgets for both long-term and annual programming. Some large firms employ full- or part-time training managers who are responsible for identifying necessary resources and developing a budget. In other firms, each department or office sets its budget. Regardless, the plan must clarify the process and may also identify major investment components.

A strategic professional development plan is likely to include only conceptual budgets for such items, or it may present a simple formula that the firm uses to set general direction. FreemanWhite's strategic educational plan, for example, states an investment goal of 4 percent of annual revenues to staff professional development. Although such ambitious goals are rare in architecture firms, identification of a strategic "set-aside" for internal learning is increasingly common.

The strategic professional development plan should also address the firm's approach to measuring return on investment. Many of the educational goals that are presented at the beginning of the firm's learning plan will, of course, reflect anticipated benefits to the firm. For example, recall Firm ABC, mentioned earlier as wishing to serve the public school market: If one of ABC's professional development goals was to improve staff understanding of trends in public school design, ABC might develop a series of workshops that introduced trends and their ramifications on classroom design. To measure the benefit of the workshops, ABC could subsequently review design development documents within a certain timeframe to determine the extent to which design solutions incorporated the newly introduced trends. Or the firm might conduct client interviews before and after the workshops.

Some firms decide to generate income from their continuing education efforts. Their professional development plans set revenue goals arising from the recruitment of tuition-paying staff from other firms, education-related software development, subleasing of in-house training facilities, and/or the provision of train-the-trainer workshops or professional development consulting services to other organizations.

The strategic learning plan should identify the human and financial investment the firm intends to make in professional development, as well as the terms and/or metrics it will use to measure potential return on investment.

6. *Designing and Implementing Activities*

The plan explains the firm's general approach to learning and its system for developing individual learning activities. The approach described in FreemanWhite's plan focuses on implementation of an "academy" and provision for individual initiatives. The Lukmire Partnership (see Figure 2.6), a much smaller architecture firm, preferred to start with vendor lunch-and-learn sessions, and it called for introduction of one additional learning vehicle and expanded system each year for four years. Gensler melds firmwide opportunities with initiatives created by individual offices; it also stimulates more learning through internal seminars and task forces and through its highly regarded mentor program than through core courses or curricula.

Few firms enjoy the luxury of dedicated training staff to take on the design of professional development activities. Consultants sometimes provide expertise and concentration for new or major professional development modules, but most firms rely on task forces and internal champions to prepare specific learning activities. The strategic professional development plan briefly explains the process through which activities are designed and the system through which they are delivered.

7. *Evaluating and Improving Activities*

Finally, the plan should mention the benchmarks or criteria the firm will use to measure success, and the process through which results will be translated into improvement.

Many firms use some of the same evaluation processes that helped them identify needs. For example, if information collected through a client satisfaction survey helped to benchmark the firm's performance and shape the learning program, then the firm might decide to conduct another survey after 24 to 36 months to measure the degree to which client perceptions had changed. Or, if a focus group of managers had determined the most critical skills for improvement, then that same focus group could convene a year or so later to discuss improvements. Firms launching their first professional development program may want to identify metrics, or measurable results. Comparing annual rates for such things as staff turnover, change orders, insurance costs, and/or profitability are easily tracked as trends.

Less quantitative, but as legitimate, are success criteria such as morale, receptiveness to change, creativity, and the like. Valuable qualities in a design firm, and often crucial to the firm's personality, such attitudes and characteristics are difficult to measure, but may be observed. For example, Rosser International has developed an internal survey process for charting progress on the extent to which staff members experience the firm's guiding principles (see Chapter 3). Trust, creativity, candor, and empowerment are among the principles covered in the survey. Other firms may rely on focus groups or managers' observations to determine change.

The plan also highlights the means by which the program will be modified and enhanced regularly, not just in response to feedback from evaluations, but also to reflect opportunities and innovative ideas generated outside the professional development program. The plan, and the professional development program, must be designed for adaptability to unanticipated learning and spontaneous bright ideas.

The Plan: Form

There is no template for a professional development plan. Plans will vary depending on the culture, objectives, and resources of individual firms. But here are a few suggestions, based on successful plans created by a range of firms:

> *Keep it short.* Brevity is the soul of anyone's reading, understanding and following the plan. Try to limit the plan to no more than one graphic or three sentences for each of the seven items presented in this chapter.

> *Graphics are good.* Arrows are really good, especially when it comes to linking the firm's business plan to the educational plan.

> *Think PowerPoint.* If the plan can be presented to a large group of people as slides, it is likely to focus on key points.

> *Remember the first principle.* People can grasp the professional development process when they see it as a cycle that includes all five elements. Perhaps there are other elements unique to your firm.

The Lukmire Partnership: A Succinct Five-Year Plan

A 25-person architecture firm in Arlington, Virginia, The Lukmire Partnership recognized that its efforts at professional development were an investment. In 1999, the firm set out to create a more formalized approach to professional development. Two simple goals were identified: set an educational direction, and make the most of limited resources. A four-person committee charged by the president quickly determined that it needed to map out a five-year plan that would:

> Meet the AIA's continuing education requirements for 18 learning unit hours per year.

> Provide professional staff with "fun and interesting ways to learn new things and expand existing knowledge."

> Focus on topics offering the most useful and current information to staff for the benefit of clients and the public at large.

> Expand the firm's general knowledge through increased sharing by in-house experts.

> Tap and share the individual experience of all professional staff.

The demands of day-to-day practice led the committee to the realistic conclusion that the first year of the plan should be devoted to preparation and planning. In the second year, it envisioned a series of lunch-and-learn sessions, provided by both internal and external experts. Year 3 would see the addition of structured half-day workshops and site visits. Year 4 would incorporate self-directed learning projects. In the fifth year, the committee felt that enough feedback and evaluative data would have been accumulated to support a full, informed strategic educational planning effort. Lukmire's grounded, yet creative, approach earned it a special citation during the 2000 AIA/CES Awards for Excellence Program.

The professional development plan for your firm should reflect its specific business framework, system for supporting innovation, and cultural attributes—in short, its competitive advantages.

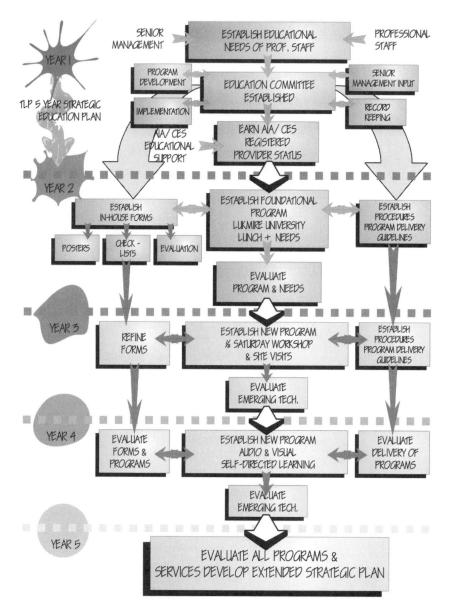

Figure 2.6 The Lukmire Partnership's five-year strategic educational plan.
©2000 Richard J. Pinskey.

Assessing Learning Strategy

Because this is a book about lifelong learning, it can't possibly go much further without some sort of quiz. In this case, the spotlight shines on the extent to which a learning strategy is manifested in your firm's activities. Does your professional development program support the firm's long-range goals? Do your educational activities reflect a strategic approach to learning? Is your program continually assessed and enhanced?

Ask yourself a few questions: To how many of the following questions can you answer "yes"? The more positive answers, the more effective your program is likely to be in helping the firm achieve its mission.

Y/N

____ 1. Does your firm have a written strategic plan for educating staff?

____ 2. Does the top management of your organization have a regular process for receiving, reviewing, and critiquing evidence of the effectiveness of your professional development program?

____ 3. Does your firm have tools and systems for regularly assessing the knowledge and skills that your staff need in order to achieve the firm's long-range goals?

____ 4. Is mentoring effectiveness a criterion for promotion to leadership positions in your firm?

____ 5. Are project managers required to conduct lessons-learned sessions during projects for the accumulation of knowledge and the identification of opportunities to improve performance?

___ 6. Do the approach and content of your firm's professional development program reflect the values and culture that shape the firm?

___ 7. Does the firm's educational program include processes for researching trends and gathering information about clients for the enlightenment of the firm's professional practice?

___ 8. Does the firm regularly research and study new information relating to health, safety, and welfare matters for the public at large?

___ 9. Does your firm have a process for identifying educational partners outside the firm?

___ 10. Does your firm have a system for regularly comparing your investment in professional development with your return on that investment?

Mavericks and Sole Proprietors

The learning dynamic is as powerful for a maverick as it is for a firm. What one knows is constantly refreshed and transformed by what one continues to learn in practice. And that new knowledge enhances one's ability to serve clients, perpetuating the dynamic.

Insider Paul Goldberger, Honorary AIA: The Challenge of Learning

Paul Goldberger, Hon. AIA and architectural critic of The New Yorker *magazine, is recognized more as a teacher through his writing than as a student. But, in order to be an effective journalist, he must be able to learn as he proceeds, to modify his approach, maybe even to change his thesis as he researches a project. Recently, Goldberger spoke about the challenge of learning.*

As years pass, it can be easy to do things by rote. We all like to keep dancing to the music we first heard. It's human nature to respond to what is familiar and comfortable. But it's essential to listen to new music, if I can continue that metaphor, even if you're not so automatically receptive to it in the way you once were. Of course it gets harder as you get older, in part because you have the weight of all of those years of dancing to the old music—or, in my case, all those years of looking at the work of architects you have known all your life. I am constantly aware of how important it is that I not let these familiar presences squeeze new people and their ideas out of my line of vision.

The greatest danger is when we believe we know all that needs to be known, that we have answers. I have never believed in overarching, all-explaining theories, and I think that helps, because I am less inclined to try to fit everything into some predetermined view of reality. And I love fresh stimulation, which counts for a lot in compensating for the fact that one doesn't automatically drift toward the new, the way you do when you are young. So, perhaps, one does have a relatively short attention span. Of course, for all the importance I place in a critic's paying close attention to what's going on now, we also have to be careful that we don't mindlessly pursue the current thing. Pretending to be 25 years old when you're twice that age is grotesque. I think the best word is "receptive." Ideally, we should all be forever 25 in our willingness to hear new ideas; at the same time, we want to explore those ideas with the benefit of an experienced and knowledgeable perspective.

As an architectural critic I have to keep an openness to new things and combine that with the knowledge I have accumulated over time. If you can't put the new into some kind of context, then there is no point to anything, and there is nothing that makes you different from someone who is 25. It's essential for me and for all of us to have a sense of memory and a sense of possibility in broad terms. Balancing the two—memory and possibility—is the key. As you move on in life, you have more memory, but you always have to hold onto a sense of possibility—to seek it, if necessary. That is one thing that has always astonished me about an architect like Philip Johnson, who for 70 years has gone to the new like a bloodhound. He is now 95, and he started paying attention to the new in the 1920s, when he helped discover the developing modern architecture in Europe of the International Style, and he still pays attention to what younger architects are doing, seeing new possibilities. I think all architects, like all architecture critics, have to balance memory and possibility—be always alert to the new, but absorbing and interpreting it through the prism of experience.

Setting out to "balance memory and possibility" is an intriguing way for any professional to approach learning and knowledge building. Planning and deliberation sometimes increase the benefit both to designers and to clients.

A personal learning plan can make a big difference. The designer who decides to improve communication and leadership skills adds value to clients, as does one who plans to focus on design, project management, or CADD. Clients require increasingly broad, deep, and diverse capabilities. Sole proprietors and professionals who chart a thoughtful professional development course within a firm, or through several firms, are likely to enjoy more satisfying and rewarding careers than peers who simply adapt to events.

So, why not take a thoughtful quiz that probes personal strategy?

Assessing Learning Strategy: Mavericks

Do your professional development efforts support your long-range goals? Do you review your learning activities in terms of their actual contribution to your professional growth and effectiveness?

Ask yourself a few questions: To how many of the following questions can you answer "yes"? The more positive answers, the likelier you are to reap the greatest benefit from the time you can devote to learning activities.

Y/N

____   1. Do I know what form of professional practice is most appropriate to my interests and values?

_____ 2. Have I objectively identified my talents and skills?

_____ 3. Have I set my professional goals for the short and long terms?

_____ 4. Have I identified the type of clients who generally provide me with projects that are most successful in both my eyes and theirs?

_____ 5. Have I determined what I should learn (about) in order to capitalize on my talents, better serve my favorite clients, and reach my goals?

_____ 6. Do I have a system for staying abreast of new health, safety, and welfare matters?

_____ 7. Do I ensure that I am exposed to fresh ideas and opportunities for innovation?

_____ 8. Have I set benchmarks for my professional growth and satisfaction? Do I take the time to think about them?

_____ 9. Do I make a point of learning from my work with clients, consultants, and vendors? Do I reflect on what I have done and observed?

_____ 10. Do I love my work?

Assessment

3

Chapter 1 explained the critical need for a design firm to secure its competitive position in the marketplace by developing a proprietary learning program, and Chapter 2 introduced the elements of an effective program and championed the first element, *strategy*. Having defined the firm's competitive attributes, established its long-range goals, and developed a clear educational strategy, it's time for the second element, *assessment*.

Assessment highlights learning gaps, areas in which expertise and knowledge are insufficient to meet the firm's objectives, and it spotlights learning opportunities, areas in which further exploration and research might boost the firm's effectiveness to a substantially higher plane. Both are important; unfortunately, the latter effort typically lags far behind the former. Firms skew continuing education programs so dramatically toward correcting deficiencies that positive activities like research and development are sacrificed year after year to basic remediation.

If the assessment process itself is deliberately conceived, objectively executed, and institutionalized as an integral feature of the professional development enterprise, assessment is more likely to be balanced,

Key Point
Assessment should spotlight learning opportunities, as well as deficiencies.

Figure 3.1 The assessment element. ©2002 Blackridge, Ltd.

to be as alert to opportunities as to deficiencies. And, to feed the learning dynamic introduced in the Chapter 2 (refer back to Figure 2.2), assessment should consider the firm, its staff, and its clients' world.

The Assessment Pyramid

A design firm is so complex and so rich in technical, interpersonal, and management challenges that identifying learning needs and opportunities is almost too easy. What do architects need to know to create tomorrow's built environment? Everything. The goal for a proprietary professional development program is, however, to enhance the knowledge base of the firm in a way that serves the firm, its clients, and staff. And so the firm begins by determining the kinds of knowledge and skills that will benefit its constituencies.

A convenient way to think about assessment priorities is as a pyramid. The most critical source of

Figure 3.2 Assessment Pyramid. © 2002 Blackridge, Ltd.

information about the firm's learning opportunities and needs forms the base. From a competitive standpoint, as discussed in Chapters 1 and 2, the most critical source of information is the firm's own long-range plan and competitive characteristics. Additional sources layer on top, providing a rich understanding of the firm's total learning potential.

Firm's Long-Range Plan

A design firm's long-range plan may be a formal document, complete with mission statement, vision, conceptual goals, a set of supporting strategies, and an annual review and modification process to keep the whole thing on track; or the plan may be a design philosophy and a set of values that are clear in the minds of the founding principals, patently obvious in the firm's activities, but seldom verbalized. Regardless of the form through which the firm's intentions become clear, its professional development program should expedite success. So assessment begins with an investigation of the firm's professional aspirations and business goals for clues about the skills, abilities, knowledge, and perspectives that will propel the firm in the right direction.

Whether one is reading documents or interviewing firm leaders, the investigation means researching the fundamental tenets of the firm's practice and looking for the answers to questions that consider the future as well as the present.

In the absence of a written long-range plan, or to confirm key elements of a formal document, education planners can ask themselves the following questions, confirm their answers with others in the firm, and look for decisions and actions that have corroborated the answers in recent months.

Where Are We Going?

- How does the firm define design excellence?
- What are the firm's core values and "personality?"
- How will the firm continue to foster innovation?
- How does the firm approach project management and design?
- Who are the firm's desired clients?
- Which services does the firm provide now and want to provide in the future?
- How does the firm wish to provide value to clients?
- How does the firm wish to contribute to society?
- What is the firm's desired culture?
- Where does the firm want to work?
- How are staff recruited and developed?
- What is the firm's attitude about growth and expansion?

- What kind of legacy does the firm wish to leave?
- Which customs, rituals, history, and lore should be passed on as part of the firm's heritage?
- What are the firm's intentions regarding ownership transition?

The answer to any of these questions has implications for the firm's professional development opportunities and needs. Design philosophy, for example: A small firm that practices locally and prizes its responsiveness to the region's specific vernacular and history might see a need to develop staff knowledge about the region's natural and cultural history and the kinds of materials and construction methods most appropriate to the area. A firm specializing in historic preservation might additionally address staff research skills.

A firm's definition of design excellence affords another example. An organization that is committed to designing distinctive institutional spaces that engage visitors on a visceral level will identify very different learning opportunities for its staff from a firm that stakes its reputation on designing workplaces dedicated to enhancing users' ability to operate efficiently.

Management and marketing plans also point toward learning needs and opportunities. If a long-range plan includes an ownership transition, then leadership development, team building, and communications will probably be in the firm's continuing education plan. Commitment to a new market or new service indicates a steep learning curve and investment in knowledge building.

When FreemanWhite (FWI) adopted the "narrow and deep" strategy discussed in Chapter 2, it reviewed what it already knew about three client types (health care, justice, and senior living), and determined that each market would benefit from services beyond those typically provided by design firms. As a result, in addition to facilities design, FWI committed to providing services in strategic positioning and workflow analysis to each client base. Charting a way to synthesize the knowledge FWI already had, to build additional knowledge, and to share knowledge among staff helped shape the firm's professional development program.

Even a firm's culture, as ephemeral as it may seem, can be studied to uncover learning opportunities. At Rosser International, part of the firm's corporate strategy is to "provide an environment that attracts and nurtures a talented, creative, and diverse workforce." Several years ago, the firm's training director reviewed the strategy and proposed a survey of all employees to determine the degree to which such guiding principles were actually experienced as part of everyday work (see Figure 3.3). The information was so useful that the survey is now updated and distributed annually. It informs not only the firm's professional development efforts, but almost every other aspect of activity as well.

As an alternative to a survey, a "town meeting," convened as an open office discussion and brainstorming event, could also engage the entire firm in considering ways that professional development might link the firm's stated vision and its pursuit of strategic goals to daily work. In any case, to position a firm competitively in the marketplace, the firm's own long-range plan must serve as the primary source for determining the aptitudes, attitudes, and knowledge that staff will need in the future.

Discipline _____ Location Code 10 20 30 40
                                                    50 90 (Circle One)

Survey of Guiding Principles of Rosser International

Column #1   Personally agree with the principle (This how you feel about the principle, not to the extent you practice.)
              Scoring: 0 (strongly disagree) to 5 (strongly agree)
Column #2   Organization as a whole practices principles
              Scoring: 0 (strongly disagree) to 5 (strongly agree)
Column #3   Division or office practices principles
              Scoring: 0 (strongly disagree) to 5 (strongly agree)

Principles	#1	#2	#3
1. I /We listen to and are accountable to clients.	___	___	___
2. I/We keep our promises to clients and stand behind the quality of service.	___	___	___
3. I/We maintain the highest level of personal integrity in all areas of work.	___	___	___
4. I/ We am/are ethical in my/our work performance.	___	___	___
5. I/We empower people to take initiative at the lowest appropriate level.	___	___	___
6. I/We bestow the authority and responsibility coupled with accountability on the individuals I/we lead.	___	___	___
7. I/We operate our company to achieve acceptable levels of profit.	___	___	___
8. I/We operate our company and serve our clients through creative ideas.	___	___	___
9. I /We are using the latest proven technology.	___	___	___
10. I/We team with our customers, our industry, and each other on the basis of trust.	___	___	___
11. I/We respect each other.	___	___	___
12. I/We pursue personal development.	___	___	___
13. I/We recognize the accomplishments of others.	___	___	___
14. I/We communicate openly.	___	___	___
15. I/We communicate clearly.	___	___	___
16. I/We communicate promptly.	___	___	___
17. I/We communicate honestly and with respect.	___	___	___
18. I/We promote an equal opportunity environment.	___	___	___
19. I/We value the strength diversity brings to our workforce.	___	___	___
20. I/We embrace change with an open mind and a willing attitude.	___	___	___ [1]

Figure 3.3 Rosser International's Survey of Guiding Principles.
© Rosser International, Inc., 1998.

Clients/Markets

The second most critical source for information about learning needs and opportunities is clients. In his role as AIA's Resident Fellow in Marketplace Research, Richard Hobbs pointed out, "By looking at the marketplace, you can define the value to be provided, which in turn defines the knowledge you need to benefit the marketplace" (*AIArchitect*, April 2001). To attract and serve your preferred clients—"preferred" having been defined in the firm's long-range plan—firms can study:

- ► Their success in serving clients
- ► Trends in the client's organization
- ► Their client's evolving markets

One way that firms gather insights about their success in serving clients is through project feedback. HOK, one of the world's largest design firms, obtains client critiques through several processes, one of which is telephone interviewing. Project managers activate the interview process at their discretion following project closeout. The interviewer, a member of the firm's in-house university, speaks with a number of the client's representatives, such as the facilities director, corporate space planner, user, and real estate manager. The HOK University representative transcribes the information, confirms it with the clients, shares it with the PM, and processes it for use by HOKU in assessing continuing education needs.

Telephone interviews are easy to conduct by firms of any size, as are site visits to completed and occupied projects; likewise, client lunches and concise email and paper surveys can provide information about client opinions and trends. And an increasingly popular way to gather substantial data is through a formal client satisfaction survey. For this, the firm retains specialist consultants to design a survey, conduct it, analyze the data, and report findings. The survey may involve personal meetings with clients or prospective clients, telephone interviews, or a paper/email process, and can engage a modest or large number of clients. In addition to investigating client perceptions about the firm's strengths and weaknesses, such surveys often research trends in the client's market. Recommendations following client satisfaction surveys might point not only to professional development opportunities, but also to such initiatives as new services, new design standards, new project management processes, and countless other administrative and operational matters that would more closely align the firm to clients.

Information gathered directly from a firm's most valued clients is enhanced when it is combined with market data available through broader sources. Most clients' professional societies and trade associations perform research, publish magazines and newsletters, conduct conferences, and willingly share market data and publications with associate members and the public at large. Local, national, and international press distribute market information on their Web sites as well as through their periodicals. Public and private universities frequently accommodate public use of their libraries and reference materials, and institutions typically sell journal subscriptions to anyone who is interested.

Design firms can easily accumulate data about where clients are headed in the future. To capitalize on the learning dynamic, a firm must consciously and constantly study emerging client trends and

 Tip

Clients expect lots of questions during the programming phase. But asking questions is not the only way to increase your understanding of their world. Clients typically appreciate genuine interest about their issues at any time. Sometimes, a simple, open-ended question elicits provocative insights. You could ask clients, or prospective clients, some of the following:

➤ What new demands are your customers placing on you?

➤ How is your organization's long-range business plan likely to change over the next five years?

➤ What is the greatest challenge facing your organization?

➤ What is the top source of information about market trends in your industry?

➤ Which trends are affecting the way you and your colleagues think about physical facilities?

Key Point

Architects know full well that almost any trend or significant occurrence will sooner or later affect practice. For the benefit of the firm, they can deliberately think about the potential ramifications of such occurrences on the firm's knowledge-building activity.

assess their implications on knowledge building and staff development. The ability to contribute to clients in the future depends on understanding where they are going.

External Signals

Competitive edge demands that a design firm's assessment for professional development opportunities begin with its mission and its contribution to clients, and then consider the universe. Architects know full well that almost any trend or significant occurrence will sooner or later affect practice. For the benefit of the firm, they can deliberately think about the potential ramifications of such occurrences on the firm's knowledge-building activity.

Insider Andy Vazzano, AIA:

The Leadership Forum at SmithGroup

The Leadership Forum is a SmithGroup program that was organized in 1999 to connect talented young staff members with the firm's top management and to research fresh ideas, abilities, and perspectives that merited introduction to the firm. The firm, in essence, combined a needs assessment process with a mentoring activity. Andy Vazzano, managing director of SmithGroup Michigan, leads the pilot program in Detroit for people with 3 to 7 years with the firm, in preleadership roles in the office.

SmithGroup has established a Leadership Forum program as an organized effort to expose emerging leadership candidates to top management, to current operations of the firm, and to evaluation approaches for new activities. Started in 1999, and now engaged with a third class, the program has been very successful.

The forum is a two-year program. The syllabus for each year has its own distinct format. During the first year, each class—usually 12 to 15 individuals who have been nominated by discipline directors—organizes into groups and undergoes a formal program of group research on a particular topic. Their work involves independent reading on the subject, followed by a presentation to management on new ideas that they think have potential application to the firm's operations and best practices. Concurrently, top management is assigned the same reading.

Specific board members make a corresponding presentation to the leadership class on current firm practices for discussion and evaluation by the class.

In her first year of the forum, Patti Brandes was very appreciative of the interactive, multilevel process. "I feel that what you learn by being told, you will learn better by reading. And what you learn by reading, you will learn better through teaching to others. As freshmen in the program, we are given the opportunity to teach and to be taught through the process of reading relevant books and then presenting the pertinent information contained within the books with our fellow forum members. Through the ensuing discussions with peers and members of the board, we learn how the theories presented apply to our company. In exchange for our effort in these presentations, board members share information with us that helps us develop a deeper understanding of the dynamics of the company."

The assigned books have direct practice application and address universal topics of interest to management principals. Books in the program have included *Zapp! The Lightning of Empowerment: How to Improve Productivity, Quality, and Employee Satisfaction* (Harmony Press, 1988) by William C. Byham with Jeff Cox, *The New Strategic Selling* (Warner Books, 1998) by Stephen E. Heiman and Diane Sanchez with Tad Tuleja, and *Managing the Professional Services Firm* (Free Press, 1997) by David H. Maister.

Year 2 of the program is formatted around more directed study and individual interface with middle management leaders. This class attends various management meetings on studio operations, marketing, leadership training, and a formal board meeting. One annual program conducted by President and CEO, Carl Roehling, offers training on marketing and client relationships, and gives the class practice on realistic client scenarios in a workshop setting.

At their choice, class members also interface with discipline and studio leaders in observing specific management tasks such as organizing an interview, directed research, participating in professional society committee meeting, or structuring a fee proposal work session. As part of SmithGroup's self-funded research initiatives, I led a project called Lab 2020, in which we interviewed scientists from around the country. We were looking for emerging scientific trends that would impact the planning and design of research facilities of the future. This was an excellent opportunity to involve year 2 forum members in direct client interface, in the documentation of new issues, in directed research activities, and in shared learning.

SmithGroup has recognized Forum as one of the best practices for generating new ideas in the firm. We will be implementing the program in all eight offices in the coming years.

Newspapers, magazines, books, radio, television, and the Internet provide more than enough general information about social, political, and economic trends. More easily applied to design firms are the insights that architectural futurists, design conference keynoters, and the architectural press share about their understanding of relevant national and international occurrences and the impact they will have on practice. The mission of schools of architecture, professional associations like the AIA, and design critics includes knowledge sharing and research. As a result, local design schools and association chapters are good places to discover issues and trends that are fodder for the firm's learning program.

For the majority of firms, gathering insights closer to home is more directly beneficial. Professional consultants, builders, and vendors who know the firm can suggest knowledge-building opportunities and needs based on their experience with the firm, with competitors, and with a greater array of clients. Similarly, business advisors—insurance companies, accountants, attorneys, management consultants—have different and valuable perspectives on the firm's strengths and weaknesses, as well as on the marketplace in general. Market research and independent image surveys can unearth information about competitors—the firms you currently run into on the interview circuit and those with which you would like to be compared—and suggest areas for staff development. And any of them might point to new markets that require new skills.

Health, safety, and welfare (HSW) issues generate urgent learning needs, as do new codes, annual state licensing criteria, certification processes, and the like. Clarity on requirements is essential for protecting professional qualifications and licenses. When in doubt, needs assessment should probably reflect the most conservative agency or state with demands, like HSW, that affect the firm's professional staff. (The American Institute of Architects is a good resource for topics that generally fall under the HSW banner as defined by state licensing boards.) Needs assessment should always include annual review of current standards.

Finally, requirements for membership, or advancement, in professional associations often specify learning accomplishments. For example, the AIA's standards for lifelong learning, mandated in 1997, dramatically and directly affected what its members define as "need-to-know." As part of its assessment process, FreemanWhite encapsulated the mandatory continuing education requirement of its diverse staff in a chart, shown in Figure 3.4.

Whatever the parameters of the design firm's business universe, leaders should consider the world beyond the firm and its clients when targeting learning opportunities.

Performance

The fourth tier of the pyramid is performance. Learning programs must respond to the firm's internal performance goals and current issues.

Each area of practice—design, operations, finance and administration, marketing, technology, research and development, professional development, and human resources—sets its own success scale.

- ▶ *Design* might look to awards and publications as evidence of achievement.
- ▶ Budget versus actual, schedule management, and number of change orders are typical

 Tip
Thomas Stewart suggests that a good question for organizations to consider is: "What emerging technologies or skills could undermine the value of our proprietary knowledge?"

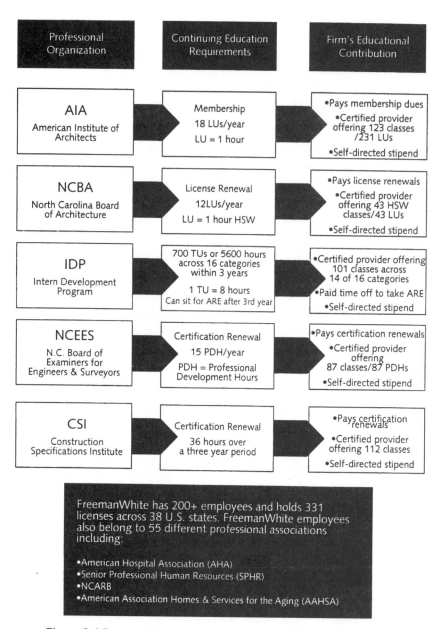

Professional Organization	Continuing Education Requirements	Firm's Educational Contribution
AIA American Institute of Architects	Membership 18 LUs/year LU = 1 hour	•Pays membership dues •Certified provider offering 123 classes /231 LUs •Self-directed stipend
NCBA North Carolina Board of Architecture	License Renewal 12LUs/year LU = 1 hour HSW	•Pays license renewals •Certified provider offering 43 HSW classes/43 LUs •Self-directed stipend
IDP Intern Development Program	700 TUs or 5600 hours across 16 categories within 3 years 1 TU = 8 hours Can sit for ARE after 3rd year	•Certified provider offering 101 classes across 14 of 16 categories •Paid time off to take ARE •Self-directed stipend
NCEES N.C. Board of Examiners for Engineers & Surveyors	Certification Renewal 15 PDH/year PDH = Professional Development Hours	•Pays certification renewals •Certified provider offering 87 classes/87 PDHs •Self-directed stipend
CSI Construction Specifications Institute	Certification Renewal 36 hours over a three year period	•Pays certification renewals •Certified provider offering 112 classes •Self-directed stipend

FreemanWhite has 200+ employees and holds 331 licenses across 38 U.S. states. FreemanWhite employees also belong to 55 different professional associations including:

•American Hospital Association (AHA)
•Senior Professional Human Resources (SPHR)
•NCARB
•American Association Homes & Services for the Aging (AAHSA)

Figure 3.4 FreemanWhite mandatory continuing education units (CEUs).

operational indicators. Hillier, headquartered in Princeton, New Jersey, uses an independent quality assurance review of all major deliverables as a source of feedback about learning needs. At other firms, project visits scheduled for 12 or 18 months postoccupancy can point both to needs ("We need to pay more attention to rooftops") and opportunities ("They seem to be pulling extra seating into most of the labs. What's changed in the way they work in those areas?").

➤ *Financial and administrative* reports on profitability, collections, overtime, overhead, as well as liability insurance premiums, legal fees, and the like, provide glaringly clear metrics that can help set continuing education priorities. The role of designers and the expectations of their clients are so broad, however, that relying on quantitative data as the compass for pointing the firm toward appropriate professional development priorities is shortsighted. Financial indicators are important, but firms are inclined to use them to spotlight deficiencies, throwing opportunities into deeper shadow and telling only half the story.

➤ The firm's performance in *marketing*—publishing, speaking, and teaching engagements; successful and unsuccessful project pursuits; award and competition entries; proposal hit rates; marketing plan benchmarks; marketing budgets; and public service ventures—suggests almost as many continuing education initiatives as do the substantial indicators described within the second tier of the pyramid.

➤ *Technology* translates into such an array of learning needs and opportunities that the challenge isn't pinpointing them; it's summarizing and ranking them. The potential of technology mushrooms incrementally each year, or so it seems to architecture firm comptrollers. Information, communication, and design technology merit attention as both subjects, and instruments, of professional development.

▶ *Research and development* is also included in the performance layer and wields even more power in learning assessment. Always implicit in the design process, R&D is increasingly recognized, embraced, and institutionalized as firms investigate construction materials, sustainable design, workflow analysis, and the like. (See the "Mavericks and Sole Proprietors" section in this chapter for an example.) Architects are publishing more books and papers than ever before, and are as likely to be speakers at client conferences as they are to be guests or exhibitors. At Shepley Bulfinch Richardson and Abbott (SBRA), one of the country's longest lived architecture firms, the role of the Technical Resources group suddenly morphed in 1994 to include formal research and development initiatives, when the group director discovered that five different project teams in the office were simultaneously researching epoxy terrazzo flooring. Research is now formalized, and SBRA conducts its own studies, supplements them with work from external specialists, and teams with clients, builders, and manufacturers to develop new materials and systems. By controlling and recording the R&D process and documenting results, SBRA's Technical Resources group suggests learning opportunities and conducts seminars for the firm's continuing education program, in addition to supporting design teams.

➤ Most obvious among the performance areas that suggest learning opportunities is *professional development*. Once in place, the firm's proprietary learning enterprise generates its own assessment benchmarks, as addressed in Chapter 9, and it makes its own contribution to the firm's performance.

➤ *Human resource* topics earn an exclusive tier on the Assessment Pyramid, *staff review*, and are discussed in the next section.

Staff Review

The fact that staff review sits so high on the pyramid, within the smallest box, is not meant to belittle human resource matters as indicators of learning opportunities. After all, the entire point of professional development is to provide people with the knowledge and skills that will facilitate their peak performance. The position and size of the box are, rather, meant to reflect the fact that the firm's mission, markets and clients, position within the external environment, and business performance standards must influence the parameters within which staffing is reviewed.

That point having been made, one observes, alas, that most firms do indeed focus their assessment efforts right here. As the president of a northeastern architecture and engineering firm succinctly and candidly put it, "We start the assessment process by looking at staff performance and by asking staff what they want to learn about, because it's the easiest way to start." True enough. But an unfortunate result of relying solely on staff performance data is that the firm could end up exerting more of its energy in fixing short-term needs than in capitalizing on knowledge-building opportunities.

With that caveat in mind, there are many ways to determine what staff should know. Both the means and form for focusing on staff vary from firm to firm, depending largely on each firm's culture. Common assessment tools include *job descriptions, internally generated staff preference surveys, externally administered preference* or *employee attitude surveys,* and *focus groups and retreats.*

Job Descriptions

Job descriptions offer direct insight to individual staff needs. Architecture and planning firm NBBJ, recipient of the 1998 AIA Continuing Education System large firm Award for Excellence, makes a direct connection between job descriptions and educational assessment. Each position requires a certain skill set, and the staff performance review process includes evaluation of those skills, as well as establishment of professional development goals for improvement, when necessary, and advancement, when appropriate.

The federal government's proclivities for assessment systems and for information dissemination combine to provide a handy model for relating learning needs to job descriptions. NASA's *Professional Development Guide* includes "Career Development Models" to help employees chart career paths. Among the models, the Project Manager Development Program (PMDP) (http://appl.nasa.gov/resources/pmpd) relates effectively to design firms. PMDP identifies several levels of project management prowess and 10 "competency categories." Some of them, such as "technical performance," "risk management," and "individual and team effectiveness," are directly transferable to design firm roles; others suggest atypical performance criteria, like "project life-cycle development." NASA project managers can log on to the Internet, determine the level that applies to them currently or prospectively, and find the competencies they must nurture for professional growth.

FreemanWhite linked assessment to formal job descriptions after the firm had encountered some resistance to its newly minted FreemanWhite Academy. Firm leaders recognized that a process for lifelong learning was essential to the organization's capability to anticipate client trends and evolve to meet them. But not everyone in the firm felt a similar passion about knowledge building and skill development. To clarify the continuing education mandate, and to make it easier for each staff member to relate the firm's goals with his or her own performance, FreemanWhite developed job descriptions for every person in the firm. Each description identifies the skills and knowledge necessary for fulfillment of the role. Using this approach, professional development is a clearly perceived means both to improving current performance and to becoming eligible for advancement within the firm.

For most firms, a basic staff performance review process can provide insights into learning needs through less formal, less integrated, study. For example, as people talk about individual skill gaps and career goals, reviewers can note repeated themes, which in turn point to continuing education opportunities for a broader audience. For even greater clarity, firms could take a lesson from Gresham, Smith and

**EXCEL**_program_

Individual Needs

List the skills required to do your job, then check the appropriate column, "Need Help" or "Do Not Need Help."

Name: _____

Job Title: _____

List of Required Skills	Need Help to Learn Basics	Need Help	Do Not Need Help
1.			
2.			
3.			
4.			
5.			
6.			
7.			
8.			
9.			
10.			
11.			
12.			
13.			
14.			
15.			

Please return to _____ by _____.

Figure 3.5 Gresham, Smith and Partners' needs assessment form.

Partners (GS&P), winner of the 2002 AIA/CES large firm Award for Excellence, in the development of its in-house training program. Part of GS&P's assessment process was to ask staff members to list their job skills and indicate the degree to which they needed help in learning or refining them (see Figure 3.5). Managers distributed the forms either to all the members of their groups or to a representative sample. Completed forms were compiled into master lists of the most frequently mentioned needs, to which managers assigned priorities.

Internally Generated Staff Preference Surveys

A second option for reviewing staff needs, internally generated staff preference surveys, dominate as the favored assessment method of design firms. These "self-surveys" range from simple, multiple-choice queries, like that in Figure 3.6, to GS&P's job-related process to full-strength professional surveys conducted by outside consultants.

In all cases, to unearth learning needs and opportunities that will enhance the firm's competitive edge, a staff survey should be designed expressly for the firm and should address topics that reflect the firm's unique mission, culture, and practice. Figure 3.6 is useful as an example of format and for ideas about content, but actual headings and topics should reflect each firm's priorities. One firm might think in terms of "business skills," as listed in the figure, whereas another office might not value "public speaking," instead thinking in terms of giving papers or making presentations to clients and/or serving on public boards. The point is, a survey should ask questions appropriate to the firm's environment.

```
┌─────────────────────────────────────────────────────────────────────┐
│                      Learning Needs Survey                            │
│                                                                       │
│  In order to understand how the firm can enhance your professional    │
│  growth, we hope you will take a few minutes to complete this         │
│  questionnaire. Please return it to _____ by 4:30 on _____.   │
│                                                                       │
│  1. What topics are especially important to you? In the first column, │
│     check all that apply. Then, in the second column, rank the 10     │
│     most important (#1 is the most important to you):                 │
│                                                                       │
│  Project Management                     Business Skills               │
│                                                                       │
│  ___ ___  Budgeting                     ___ ___  Public Speaking      │
│  ___ ___  Negotiations                  ___ ___  Business Writing     │
│  ___ ___  Managing Risk                 ___ ___  Networking           │
│  ___ ___  Change Orders                 ___ ___  Client Maintenance   │
│  ___ ___  Leading Project Meetings      ___ ___  Team Building        │
│  ___ ___  Managing Consultants          ___ ___  Leadership           │
│  ___ ___  Other:                        ___ ___  Other:               │
│  ___ ___  Other:                        ___ ___  Other:               │
│                                                                       │
│                                                                       │
│  Technical Skills                       Building Technology           │
│                                                                       │
│  ___ ___  Sketching                     ___ ___  Sustainable Design   │
│  ___ ___  AutoCad                       ___ ___  Specifications       │
│  ___ ___  Graphic Design                ___ ___  Codes                │
│  ___ ___  CD Quality                    ___ ___  Building Systems     │
│  ___ ___  3D Modeling                   ___ ___  Other:               │
│  ___ ___  Other:                        ___ ___  Other:               │
│                                                                       │
│  2. What is the best time for in-house programs? Check one:           │
│  ___  Early morning, 7 – 9 AM                                         │
│  ___  Mid-day, 11:30 AM – 1:30 PM                                     │
│  ___  Late afternoon, 4:30 – 6:30PM                                   │
│                                                                       │
│  3. If you are aware of any programs or speakers that might be        │
│     effective in addressing any of these topics, please list          │
│     relevant information below:                                       │
│                                                                       │
└─────────────────────────────────────────────────────────────────────┘
```

Figure 3.6 Simple preferences survey.

Externally Generated Surveys

Externally generated surveys, a third assessment option, offer the benefit of objectivity. Einhorn Yaffee Prescott (EYP), Architecture and Engineering, PC, retained a consulting firm to conduct an online survey that established how staff felt about their current performance, where continuing education might help them, and what their most effective learning formats would be.

The ability to do one's job well is an imperative for most design professionals, and EYP's survey stimulated employees to think about their productivity and that of people they supervised. The identification of perceived obstacles to productivity confirmed that staff desired continuing education (see Figure 3.7).

Based on these findings, it is likely that a professional development program would respond to more than the 23 percent of EYP's staff, who expressed an explicit need for continuing education. "Communication between individuals and offices" (11 percent) and "understanding the firm's goals, procedures, and practices" (19 percent) would also be facilitated by a professional development program that was designed

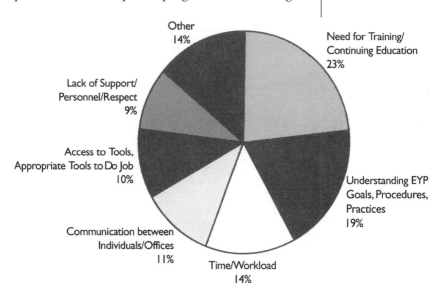

Figure 3.7 Barriers to productivity. Prepared by Monalco, Inc., for Einhorn Yaffee Prescott, Architecture and Engineering, PC.

in part to do so. In fact, when staff were asked about the areas in which they wished to grow professionally, communication was mentioned specifically, as were EYP procedures and practices (see Figure 3.8).

In addition to data about the collective learning preferences of individuals, EYP's survey expressly asked senior staff for their impressions about the situation with people who reported to them. Studio and department managers listed the top 10 learning needs concerning their groups.

Staff surveys do not necessarily address only learning preferences. Employee attitude surveys are common human resource tools that focus on the general experience people have working in the firm. Although not expressly addressing continuing education, information gathered via these instruments invariably relates to such matters as communications, delegation, resources, career growth, and pro-

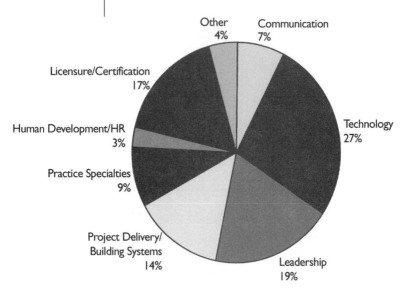

Figure 3.8 Continuing education interests in the coming year. Prepared by Monalco, Inc., for Einhorn Yaffe Prescott, Architecture and Engineering, PC.

fessional satisfaction, so staff attitude surveys also point to development opportunities within the firm.

Group Discussions

A fourth vehicle for gathering insights about what staff should know is group discussions. Focus groups engage senior managers or a cross section of staff, as a firm's culture suggests. Department or officewide town meetings assemble entire constituencies. Clients and or consultants can participate to amplify insights. No matter how large or small the group, the goal is the same: invite members of the firm to help shape the firm's learning program.

Insider Emily Nalven, with Margaret Goglia, AIA:

An Agenda for the Future: UC PMI's Direction-Setting Workshops

An institutional design and facilities department has a lot of the same requirements as a design firm: Deliver projects that respond to clients' needs, on time, on budget. Manage consultants. Find and nurture talented staff. And recognize that staff development improves project quality and client satisfaction.

Facilities design and construction professionals within the University of California face the same concerns as their counterparts who work inside design firms—actually, who work inside multiple-office design firms. Emily Nalven is the coordinator of the University's Project Management Institute (UC PMI.) Margaret Goglia, AIA, is past director of the institute, now a project leader at Lawrence Berkeley Laboratories. UC PMI used a workshop approach to needs assessment, rather like a cross between a focus group and a town meeting.

Sometimes large decentralized organizations have difficulty getting the attention and appropriate audience for voluntary, in-house training programs. This is not currently the case for the University of California's systemwide UC Project Management Institute, a staff training program targeted to UC facilities planning, design, and construction employees working across the state in 10 UC campuses, three national DOE research laboratories, and five teaching hospitals.

Managed by the Planning, Design, and Construction unit within the UC Office of the President Facilities Administration Department, UC PMI provides both

---

AIA learning units and continuing education credits to its program participants. The institute offers timely programs that are geared specifically to the University of California's capital program business practices and legal obligations. And UC PMI's commitment to offer quality programs that reflect these objectives is characterized by a service focus and participatory direction setting. But at one point, staff participation in UC PMI's voluntary program plummeted, and a collaborative approach to needs assessment revitalized it.

In 1996, following a number of successful years, UC PMI's programs suffered from low attendance and participant dissatisfaction. Concurrently, there was a UC PMI leadership change. The new UC PMI Director, Margaret Goglia, AIA, took participant dissatisfaction as an opportunity to redevelop the program, structure a new role for the position, and foster an institutional approach to in-house continuing education. A program called the Agenda for the Future was the vehicle to bring these three objectives together. Agenda for the Future was conceived as a facilitated workshop group to highlight the target participants' training needs, as well as their supervisors' views of the target participants' training needs.

Leaders of the university's capital program ($60 billion)—those who send their design and construction project managers to training and those who have a direct working relationship with facilities or project management staff—were invited to attend the initial Agenda for the Future. Workshop participants included a cross section, representing as many campus locations as possible, as well as the Office of the President. Representatives from budget, contract, project management, and senior-level staff (such as design and construction, and facilities leaders) were asked to provide their own perspective on staff training and support.

The session was designed and led by consultants who were experts in design firm professional development programming and who could provide the requisite neutral facilitation needed for frank dialogue. The objective was to have all 55 participants feel that their needs for training were acknowledged and that the uniqueness and needs of each campus would be taken into account as specific training programs were developed.

The Agenda for the Future program was quite successful in achieving its objectives. Needs were identified, people's priorities were honored, and the special nature of each campus was acknowledged. Based on the work accomplished in the session, programs could be developed easily with the target audience in mind. Information on the attitudes of relevant supervisors (those who would need to approve target audience participation) had also been gathered and could be woven into the learning objectives. The new UC PMI director had been able to meet and talk with representatives of her target audience and their supervisors to hear about their needs first-hand. The consultants were able to direct the session, provide the right neutral context for honest input, and free the new UC PMI director to engage in less structured dialogue and receive unsolicited feedback and suggestions.

Because of this success, and since the nature of the information gathered has a limited shelf life, the Agenda for the Future program was convened again in 1999 with similar valuable results.

The UC PMI does have other ways of determining the campuses' training needs from year to year: program evaluations, survey tools, and quarterly meetings of the capital program leaders (e.g., assistant vice chancellors, executive medical center directors, etc.). All of these are used in conjunction with the reports from the past Agenda for the Future workshops. As a result, formal meetings, training programs, and special-issue workshops sponsored by UC PMI are well attended by all of the campuses.

Using the Assessment Pyramid

As mentioned at the beginning of this chapter, assessment is presented as a pyramid simply to clarify that, in terms of competitive edge, the most critical sources of information about the firm's learning opportunities and needs form the base. An effective assessment is, however, not one that relies exclusively on study of the long-range plan and external factors. The best assessment process is one that considers multiple levels of the pyramid, plus some things that don't neatly fit inside the pyramid at all.

A firm just embarking on a continuing education program might decide in its first year to rely on information contained in its long-range plan and data from a staff survey to give direction to its knowledge-building activities. In year 2, it might look at results from its fledgling in-house program, as well as consider ideas from external sources, to give the program substance.

In any case, a formalized assessment process, like that suggested by the pyramid, benefits the firm in multiple ways:

- ➤ It determines learning priorities.
- ➤ It provides data that can be tapped for other practice uses beyond continuing education.
- ➤ It builds integrity into the entire professional development program.
- ➤ It provides benchmarks from which to measure success.

Mavericks and Sole Proprietors

For most practitioners, and especially for mavericks and sole proprietors, learning needs and opportunities can arise suddenly, and an immediate question can become a research project with long-lasting benefits.

Insider Peter E. Madsen, FAIA:

A Learning Need Becomes a Learning Opportunity

Peter E. Madsen, FAIA, has pursued an untraditional career path, applying his architectural training and talent to the world of commercial real estate. He is managing director of Pembroke Real Estate, Inc., a Fidelity Investments company specializing in real estate development. Before joining Fidelity in 1997, Madsen was a principal of Graham Gund Architects and president of The Gunwyn Company, an affiliated real estate development firm.

In 2001, when Pembroke ran an international competition for the design of a new multibuilding, mixed-use development in the London Docklands, several factors converged that challenged me and plunged me into an immersion process, involving investigation of a whole integrated array of new building skin and systems technologies.

My career background is comprised largely of buildings with assorted picturesque punched-opening masonry skins. Accordingly, I had seen little need to move from familiar, traditional American HVAC systems. Even recently, a similar competition

---

in Boston had produced only traditional approaches to enclosure, and our year-old London office was yet another example of this theme.

So the question arose, how to evaluate a completely different, but far more rational aesthetic, complete with chilled beams, chilled ceilings, active wall façades, klima façades, and the like? Interestingly, only one of four competition entries looked at all conventional, and even it pushed the limits of our collective experience. The concepts had been clearly presented, and they were easy enough to grasp, but the big question we kept coming back to was, "How effectively does such an approach really work?"

Driven by curiosity, I used the next few months to make extensive building tours to Germany, the Netherlands, and throughout the United Kingdom, networking contacts in the design and construction fields. I researched published material, met with facility managers, architects, and product representatives, and had group information reviews with colleagues, reporting back on each other's homework. Often some answers raised even more follow-up questions: "How do we treat the perimeter?" "How do we prevent condensation?" "How do we clean the inner surfaces of the airspace?"

Absent appropriate answers to these rather small-sounding problems, the basic system wouldn't have been satisfactory, so we had no choice but to drill down into the detail. We had to ask, ask, and ask again, until we got authoritative answers, corroborated. This type of perhaps tedious-sounding exercise was not academic for us. At Pembroke, people are personally accountable for their decisions, and the other team members and I found this pure empirical research extremely valuable. And I picked up some AIA learning units, as well.

Now about to start construction on this 1-million-square-foot facility, we are delighted with our design, pleased to have advanced technology significantly, and confident that we are delivering a superior working environment to our tenants.

And, at the moment, we're even adapting these ideas to the harsher visual and environmental climate of Boston!

As mavericks and sole proprietors think about their professional development, four simple questions can yield a wealth of information about needs and opportunities.

➤ What do you need in order to do your current work better?

➤ What could you learn about to serve clients more effectively?

- ➤ What do you need in order to advance to a higher position or gain an additional expertise?
- ➤ What could you learn about in order to be a more fulfilled professional?

As mentioned in Chapter 1, a thoughtful approach to knowledge building benefits every professional's ability to command interesting projects and achieve personal goals.

Program Planning and Design

4

With the first two elements in place, the firm has pinpointed its competitive advantages and long-range goals, developed a learning strategy, and identified learning needs and opportunities. Program planning and design comprise the next element (see Figure 4.1).

The primary goal of a firm's learning enterprise should be knowledge building, rather than information accumulation. The former relies on people, the latter depends on systems. The former is a way of life, the latter an historical resource. For information and impressions to become knowledge, someone has to reflect, synthesize, and apply them to new situations. In a design firm, knowledge is knowing what you know, using what you know, sharing what you know, and questioning what you know.

Similarly a professional development program is not just about skill building and exposure to facts, data, and experiences. Professional development is about stimulating people to assimilate, experiment, use, and share ideas, techniques, and questions. In its presentation of learning options to staff, Gensler has

Figure 4.1 The planning and design element.
© 2002 Blackridge, Ltd.

described itself as a learning organization "that is dedicated to long-term, proactive, holistic learning, rather than sporadic and reactive training to fill perceived gaps in knowledge."

Planning: Means-to-Needs

Once assessment is complete, the firm can plan ways to address learning gaps and capitalize on knowledge-building opportunities. It can think about the means it will use to address needs. *Means-to-needs*, shorthand for the process of matching a knowledge-building process to the gap or opportunity it wants to fill, requires answers to some very basic questions:

- ▶ *Why* does the firm think there is a need or opportunity for learning in this area?
- ▶ *What* is the specific subject that deserves to be addressed?

- ► *Who* should build this knowledge or skill?
- ► *How* should learning occur in this area?
- ► *How* will new knowledge or ability be *manifested*?

Why?

Let's look at an example. The ability to budget staff requirements of projects is a basic practice skill and a frequent topic for continuing education. If a subject has been identified, then there is already an answer to the "what" question. But it's also important to clarify the reason it is a matter for attention, because that reason will probably suggest a means for gaining the appropriate learning.

Budgeting is a tool for project management, so future project managers (PMs) need to be able to develop conceptual budgets, monitor them, and modify them. In this case, budgeting is a practice skill that many people need to be able to employ. In addition, they probably need to use the firm's standard process and formats for developing, updating, and managing budgets.

What?

There is some synergy between "why" and "what." Each helps clarify the other. And answers can change over time. Let's return to our example on budgeting. In order to prepare burgeoning PMs for greater responsibility, the firm decides to develop a basic program on budgeting. A few years later budgeting may again arise as a topic, but for a completely different reason: The firm's profitability is suffering, and budget development and management may be culprits. The reason is very different; the subject is slightly different; and the audience will undoubtedly

Program Planning and Design

be different. In each case, answering "what" and "why" has led to "who."

Who?

In the first scenario, future PMs need to be able to budget. In that case the audience is, minimally, a stream of young architects who aspire to project leadership. But is that the only audience? For many firms, it will be. But other offices, perhaps those that differentiate between project designers and project managers, may want the audience to include designers. Even if their designers are not responsible for managing budgets, these firms might see an advantage to having designers who are sophisticated about, and sympathetic to, budgets. Or a firm might be instituting entirely new project management software, and determine that both principals and staff need to refresh their budgeting skills. Or, as in the example of the firm with poor profitability, everyone's understanding budgeting may need to be addressed. Clarity on "why" and "who" now leads to "how."

How?

As shown in Figure 4.2, the best means for reaching all the audiences may be the same: training seminars. But a firm's specific situation at the time, and its culture, might dictate different seminars for different purposes.

Budgeting seminars for future PMs might be designed in a traditional classroom format as a series of lectures and demonstrations. The introduction of new processes for principals will likely be a one-time effort, perhaps requiring a meeting and/or individual coaching. Seminars for designers might be more conceptual and less hands-on, or they might be eliminated altogether in favor of mentoring relationships.

Why?	What?	Who?	How?[a]	How manifested[a]
PMs need to know how to prepare and manage budgets	Project staffing budgets	Future PMs Current PMs	Three-session seminar with coached practice for new PMs	1. Completed budgets 2. Timley budget vs. actual reports
Designers should be more sensitive to project parameters	Project staffing budgets and schedules	Designers Principals in charge (PICs)	1. Workshop 2. Mentoring	1. Fewer changes in CD phase 2. Fewer complaints about staff allocation
Poor profitability	Project staffing budgets	Future PMs Current PMs Project teams	Seminars Workshop Team work session	1. Completed budgets 2. Timley budget vs. actual reports 3. Accurate timecards 4. Increased profitability

[a]Numbered items pertain to all of the "Who's" in the same row.

Figure 4.2 Matching means to needs.

"How" can also suggest that the firm should look to sources outside itself to assist learning. Schools of architecture, AIA chapters, for-profit training companies, and vendors might be able to address a subject adequately at less cost.

How Manifested?

The reasons for pursuing a subject suggest their own benchmarks. "Why" leads to "how manifested." If project managers need to know how to develop and manage budgets, there are at least two ways that their new skill will be manifested: through their development of accurate budgets and through their reporting budget status as the project proceeds. The firm might also take a broad view and track profitability and staff utilization.

Program Planning and Design　　　　　　　　　　　　　**87**

As a firm plans its approach to professional development, the means-to-needs process directs attention to desired outcomes and the results of learning, as well as to the learning mechanics. By starting with an idea of how the firm will measure the success of its professional development program, the firm builds accountability into the program.

But the development of professionals involves more than just the accumulation of skills, so the ways in which learning success is manifested may be unclear at the outset. Figure 4.3 shows two more learning initiatives, one with more clearly anticipated success measures.

At this point, the firm has objectively determined learning needs and opportunities that will advance its mission and solidify its position in the marketplace. And it has planned how to address those needs and opportunities in the most effective ways. The next step will be to design a responsive knowledge-building program.

Why?	What?	Who?	How?[a]	How manifested[a]
PICs too hands-on	Delegation Communication	Principals	1. Leadership seminar 2. Coaching 3. Peer mentoring	1. Fewer PIC hours on projects 2. Increased PM satisfaction 3. Less PM turnover
Designers should be environmentally responsible	Sustainable design	Committee	1. Research and travel 2. Peer mentoring	Recommendations to principals

[a]All the numbered items pertain to "who" in the same row.

Figure 4.3 Identifying success measures.

Designing the Umbrella Program

Architects are smart, sophisticated, and passionate. They are accustomed to learning, and to learning every day. An enterprise for their professional development must be rich and textured if it is going to engage them. Firms like NBBJ craft their continuing education program to address the personal lives of employees, as well as professional needs and desires, because of the architects' devotion to their work. One description of the NBBJ learning program, for example, explains that the firm sustains its staff's high level of "enthusiasm, inspiration, and creativity" by offering a broad and flexible program for people with varying interests and different abilities (NBBJ, 1999).

To engage designers, a firm's professional development program should:

➤ Incorporate best educational practices.

➤ Facilitate internal knowledge sharing.

➤ Provide various learning methods.

➤ Organize around firm priorities.

Incorporate Best Educational Practices

Designers of in-house learning programs benefit from familiarity with trends in adult education. Whether through research and reading, education and training experts, and/or commiseration with their institutional clients, firms have a parallel profession from which to draw ideas and applications.

Educational theory suggests many approaches that are relevant to design professionals. For example, the Theory of Multiple Intelligences, developed by psychologist and educator Dr. Howard Gardner, presents ideas about how to design a program that appeals to a range of learners. Gardner observes that people have different, and multiple, "intelligences." To teach or inspire, one should create a program that reaches people on as many levels as possible. To date, Gardner has identified eight intelligences:

Verbal/linguistic	Bodily/kinesthetic
Logical/mathematical	Interpersonal
Visual	Intrapersonal
Musical	Naturalist

Common professional development formats—workshops, roundtable discussions, mentoring relationships, and others described in later chapters—appeal to *verbal, logical, visual,* and *interpersonal* intelligences. *Musical* is a bit more of a stretch, although pleasing voices, mood music, or sound effects could reinforce learning for people with acute musical intelligence. Site visits and demonstrations address *bodily* intelligence. Reflection, research, and personal action plans are the kinds of activities that engage people's *intrapersonal* intelligence. The *naturalist* intelligence would be stimulated by subjects such as landscaping and sustainable design, as well as examples and references from nature.

The education profession offers more than theories, like Multiple Intelligences, to help in designing programs. Educational agencies and boards are excellent resources. The National Architectural Accreditation Board (NAAB) reviews schools of architecture to ensure that undergraduate and graduate programs adequately prepare young people for the profession. Aspects of the board's accrediting processes and criteria can serve as useful templates for in-firm programs, starting with intern development programs and con-

Program Planning and Design

tinuing through all of the firm's continuing education programs. The way that NAAB identifies levels of student proficiency, for example, is a useful mechanism for defining learning objectives (more on this a little later in the chapter). NAAB's 37 performance criteria, starting with spoken and written verbal skills, and culminating in ethics and professional judgment, suggest program elements that continue to be as relevant for AIA fellows as they are for freshly minted graduate architects. Educational experts also provide insights into technology. Distance learning, whether modules are created in-house or purchased from training vendors, can be a powerful supplement to the firm's professional development program. Whether online or through a virtual classroom, via telephone or videoconferencing, distance learning helps accommodate staff who need flexible schedules, work from home or off-site, or are located in different offices. Participants can experience most continuing education formats, including mentoring, and firms can realize increased efficiency, flexibility, and economy. And the fact that distance learning technology accommodates both asynchronous and synchronous learning, allowing staff to participate on their own, at their own pace, or with others in real time, makes distance learning a viable option for design professionals.

Facilitate Internal Knowledge Sharing

In design firms, people learn primarily in the course of working on projects, and, typically, they share what they know on a casual, need-to-know basis. Junior staff watch in-house gurus; senior staff seek out new staff with special skills; and everyone swaps perspectives gained from conferences, committee work, and projects—if and when the mood strikes them.

To spur greater exchange among professionals, firms design professional development formats that accommodate, and stimulate, varying levels of inquiry and mastery. The full transfer of experience and wisdom from one person to another may be impossible, but when expert and novice deliberately engage, learning is facilitated, and both parties can benefit. The learner acquires a deeper understanding or greater ability; the facilitator becomes more conscious of and coherent about her or his own knowledge, hence is more likely to apply it effectively.

Training, coaching, and mentoring are three formats for knowledge transfer that work well in the framework of daily activity (see Figure 4.4):

> *Training* exposes people to something new, typically by connecting a senior staff member with junior staff in a seminar or classroom situation.

> *Coaching* helps people use what has been introduced to them; it includes observed practice, in which an expert observes and critiques a novice's performance.

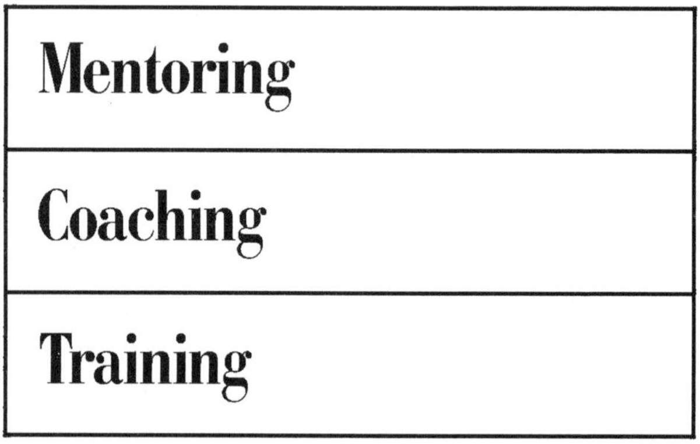

| Mentoring |
| Coaching |
| Training |

Figure 4.4 Three methods of knowledge transfer.

Program Planning and Design

► *Mentoring* leads to mastery, pairing the expert and not-so novice in a less structured arrangement, in which the expert serves as a resource and the novice deliberately tests burgeoning expertise.

Note that in the definitions of these methods, the terms *expert* and *novice* are used, rather than words like *senior staff* and *junior staff*, for the simple reason that expertise does not necessarily reside in a head of graying hair. Those of us who still smart from having to earn our computer literacy at the side of a much younger person are very aware that age has little to do with proficiency. One clever design firm instituted a mentoring process to raise understanding about sexual harassment by pairing novices—in this case, the firm's principals, all men—with appropriate experts, all younger female professionals. Similarly, a project manager experienced in university R&D facilities might have as much to learn from a younger designer specializing in biotech facilities, as the designer from the PM.

Although age is irrelevant to the relationship between a novice and an expert in an architecture firm, the knowledge-sharing format dramatically affects how novices and experts conduct themselves. Coaching raises the competency bar of the person who has been trained. Mentoring promotes even greater mastery. And the difference among the three is the relative involvement of novice and expert in a learning process (see Figure 4.5).

At the training level, knowledge is introduced. The expert shapes and presents ideas and information; novices listen and question. It's school. The trainer does most of the work, determining exactly what will be shared, who the audience will be, how

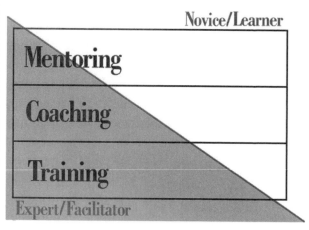

Figure 4.5 The Involvement Model. © Blackridge, Ltd.

content will be presented, and what novices will do during— and perhaps after— the engagement. Typically conducted in classroom style, training activities demand the most expert time and involvement.

Coaching is more a 50–50 relationship. The coach still designs how knowledge will be shared, but the novice participates almost equally in the learning activity. Practicing under the watchful eye of the expert, the novice is hands-on, attempting to use the information and ideas that were introduced earlier, and already adopting a personal style. When knowledge is being shared, this level is likely to be the most exciting to the novice and the most unnerving to the expert. Serving as a coach to a design professional can sometimes feel like teaching a teenager to drive. Conversely, being coached by a design professional can sometimes feel like being taught to drive by a stressed parent. Both roles are demanding.

When knowledge sharing has reached a mentoring level, the novice has absorbed almost all that the expert can provide. The novice is now responsible

 Key Point

Novices are uncomfortable lingering for very long at the training level. Thwarted from testing their own ideas, they lose interest in learning. Similarly, experts can become drained and frustrated by too much time spent at the training and coaching levels.

for using the knowledge, adapting it to new situations, adding to it, and passing it on to others, probably in a somewhat different version. Available for feedback and collaboration, the expert is involved minimally. Novice and expert have flipped involvement levels from their training mode.

Participants benefit from an evolving expert/novice partnership not only in knowledge sharing, but also in trust and autonomy. As senior members of the firm play the role of expert through each level, their trust in the abilities of novices increases. Senior staff are likelier to delegate to people they trust. Similarly, novices' new abilities position them for greater autonomy and contribution to projects and the firm.

For each level of the Involvement Model, there are effective knowledge-sharing processes that adapt comfortably to the professional setting and go beyond the experiential learning of projects. At the training level, firms develop a curriculum of workshops and seminars, or "university," taught by experts. In coaching mode, principals and project managers can adjust the project delivery process to include a "lessons learned" module, in which team members share information and insights to benefit their projects in the short term and feed into the firm's learning dynamic over time (refer back to Figure 2.2.) At the mentoring level, firms craft mentoring systems and protocols to institutionalize the knowledge of valued experts and clarify career paths for junior and senior staff.

The rate at which novices move up through the three levels varies from situation to situation and person to person. A new senior project manager may begin at the training level when he or she joins the firm, but only long enough to learn the firm's particular PM protocols and processes. A principal-in-charge may serve as coach through the new PM's first project for the firm, or may quickly switch to mentor mode, depending on the PM's facility with the firm's way of managing projects.

In any case, novices in design firms are uncomfortable lingering for very long at the training level. If they feel they are being held back, they lose interest in learning. Similarly, experts can become drained and frustrated by too much time at the training and coaching levels. The solution: variety.

Provide Various Learning Methods

Although most firms launch professional development through a single format, typically a series of courses in classroom style, they quickly realize that variety really is the spice of lifelong learning for designers. Blended learning—in which one builds knowledge through several processes—appeals to architects.

Part of the employee survey conducted by Einhorn Yaffee Prescott during its assessment phase, as discussed in Chapter 2, was devoted to discerning staff preferences for common learning methods. Although an individual's preference for a particular method will be influenced by the situation at hand, EYP staff generally preferred knowledge sharing to self-based study (see Figure 4.6).

Learning preferences are likely to vary from firm to firm, discipline to discipline, generation to generation, and, as just mentioned, from situation to situation. In addition to in-house universities, lessons-learned sessions, and mentoring relationships, there are as many options as there are preferences for the design of professional development programs.

Program Planning and Design

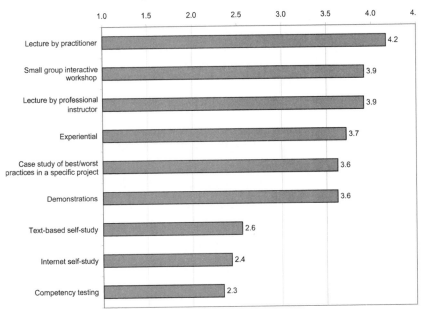

Learning Preferences
(Rated on 1-5 scale with 5=high preference)

Learning Method	Rating
Lecture by practitioner	4.2
Small group interactive workshop	3.9
Lecture by professional instructor	3.9
Experiential	3.7
Case study of best/worst practices in a specific project	3.6
Demonstrations	3.6
Text-based self-study	2.6
Internet self-study	2.4
Competency testing	2.3

Figure 4.6 Learning preferences. Prepared by Monalco for Einhorn Yaffee Prescott, Inc.

HOK, the AIA/CES 1999 large firm Award for Excellence winner, considers a range of learning opportunities for each staff level, which is reflected in the firm's Career Mapping program. For example, an entry-level professional is expected to:

- ► Understand the HOK standards for projects and project process.

- ► Develop skills in listening, writing, speaking, and presenting.

- ► Be able to work within budget, schedule, and client constraints.

- ► Understand HOK's decision-making structure.

- Learn to collaborate, take direction, and listen.
- Learn to organize and communicate ideas.
- Learn other disciplines and project processes.

Consequently, the firm provides various, and relevant, learning opportunities for entry level staff, including:

- New employee orientation
- In-house training on design, technical, and craft skills, and management
- In-house opportunities to develop skills in organization and presentation
- Site visits or equivalent roundtable project discussions
- Project meetings
- Postproject reviews
- Rotation within discipline
- Role model and mentor relationships with HOK staff member
- Access to professional journals and other relevant reading materials
- Attendance at HOK meetings, socials, brownbag lunches
- Computer training
- External seminars
- Performance appraisals

HOK's Career Mapping process similarly matches expectations and assorted development opportunities for staff at all levels, including professionals, senior professionals, project leaders, and office leaders; and it demonstrates higher expectations as staff grow. For example, while the entry-level professional is expected to learn to collaborate and take direction, a few years later at the professional level, the same designer is expected to be able to delegate and supervise. If the professional wishes to move into project management, then he or she must also demonstrate coaching skills.

Architecture firms can further expand the array of learning opportunities available to staff and gain outside perspective about program design by teaming with other continuing education providers, as did Baltimore based architecture and engineering firm RTKL. "Freedom without Fortresses: Shaping the New Secure Environment" was a symposium organized through RTKL's internal university, Forum, and co-sponsored by AIA, *Architectural Record*, and the National Building Museum. Conducted in fall 2001, following 9/11, the program was open to the public.

Architects can link to a universe of learning partners, as Thom Lowther points out in the next Insider sidebar.

Insider Thom Lowther: The Architect's Educational Universe

Thom Lowther, Ed.S., is director of the AIA Continuing Education System. An expert in professional development, Lowther came to the AIA in 1995 with 20 years experience in continuing education for the medical, legal, and accounting professions. During his tenure, he has initiated numerous CES partnering initiatives with schools of architecture, AIA chapters, materials manufacturers and suppliers, and international institutions for the benefit of the professional development of architects.

There are three key contributors to the architect's educational universe: schools and universities, practitioners, and manufacturers and professional organizations. The first contributor includes more than 110 accredited schools of architecture in the United States and Canada. Architecture schools provide a foundation of concept and theory under the guidance of such professional regulatory organizations as the National Architectural Accrediting Board and the Association of Collegiate Schools of Architecture.

The second contributor is composed of practitioners themselves, independent or working within architectural and engineering firms. Equipped with the conceptual

---

skills that they were taught in school, young architects learn on the job, quickly facing the fact that reality doesn't always fit their packages of academic theory or concept. The problem-solving skills of architects take the lead until practical applications can be learned; and strong mentoring programs and Intern Development Programs (IDP) can play a vital role in the shaping of young architects. Practicing architects are regulated by such organizations such as the National Certification and Architectural Registration Board and state licensing boards. Seasoned architects are supported by professional development programs offered by associations such as the American Institute of Architects (AIA) and the Construction Specification Institute.

The third contributor includes the vast network of product representatives and nonprofit organizations. These organizations provide the practical application of product and service education to the architects and firms. Supporting design professional organizations such as the Architectural Woodworking Institute and National Concrete Masonry Association are but a few offering quality continuing education as it applies to their niche of the industry. Another vital component that supplies up-to-date product continuing education is manufacturers. Many product suppliers, manufacturers, and trade organizations have been organized by the AIA to form the AIA Continuing Education Systems network.

The three contributors converge in architectural practice, and the degree to which they mesh has changed. Traditionally, schools of architecture provided the profession with a steady supply of raw architects equipped with problem-solving skills, but little practical knowledge. Mostly, firms had to develop graduate architects through on-the-job training. The training department of many firms consisted of manufacturers who knocked on the door with lunches and product materials for noontime discussion. The priority was lunch first, then needs. The relationship between schools of architecture and firms was adequate. The relationship between manufacturer and practitioner was limited to need and transactions. The relationship between the schools of architecture and the manufacturer was minimal at best.

Today, schools of architecture are beginning to work more closely with practitioners and firms in a joint effort, for professional development and teaching of case studies. The training department of many firms is changing, by focusing on identifying training needs and by inviting select manufacturers to provide specific training to match those needs. In this manner, the relationship between manufacturer and practitioner is transforming to become one of consultant and resource. The relationship between the schools of architecture and the manufacturer is transforming, also, into one of shared knowledge, resources, and joint continuing education opportunities.

©Thom Lowther, *The Architects' Universe*

Firms also team with each other. Large and small firms partner with their counterparts to design programs on generic topics like budgeting or CADD, so they can capitalize on each other's strengths, and conserve resources for investment in proprietary learning. Self-directed learning is another robust approach to professional development; it is addressed in the "Mavericks and Sole Proprietors" section in this chapter.

Organize around Specific Firmwide Priorities

In the best of all possible worlds, creation of the firm's program would proceed in an almost linear mode, from educational strategy to assessment to design. However, there are clients to serve and a firm to run. Moreover, design of the program should reflect where the firm is at the moment, as well as where it wants to be in the future, because staff will be more enthusiastic about participating—as authors, learners, and facilitators—in a program that reflects matters urgent to them.

When FreemanWhite created its learning program, it initially homed in on project management training as the place to begin design. One of the firm's strategic success measures is the "satisfaction clients derive from the FreemanWhite experience." PM training was a logical starting point, and one that would build integrity into the continuing education process by linking it immediately to the firm's long-range and educational visions. Improvements in project management would also affect almost everyone in the firm and stimulate awareness of the program.

Sometimes, learning design must consider factors far beyond the firm's control. Quentin Elliott, AIA, Education chair of NBBJ's award-winning Columbus program, observes that the early-1990s recession in the United States resulted in a wave of young architects abandoning the profession. Their absence continues to be felt a decade later, in the shortage of midlevel talent—in some parts of the country, as much as 20 to 40 percent less than it might have been. Elliott asserts that the resulting vacuum in firms must be filled through vigorous professional development, so NBBJ's program is designed to reach people on multiple levels. "Lunch bunches" muster staff around client-centered topics, like criminal justice and medical planning. Daylong seminars are planned quarterly for in-depth study. NBBJ's Seattle office conducts an annual 24-hour charrette, which is juried. NBBJ's program addresses development for all staff, but focuses as necessary.

Sonja Winburn, director of Human Resources and leader of Rosser International's program, is clear about the need to balance strategic educational goals and immediate practice needs. "You have to work into the firm's political climate at the time, and you must have very clear goals about what you are trying to accomplish. It must be tied to current performance problems, current business goals, and issues that are relevant. Even when we structure our program to respond to things we need to address as a matter of course, there seems always to be something that has to be done right now." Far from being disappointed about the need for flexibility, Winburn is pleased. "We end up with a system that functions the way I originally hoped. It is never static."

Designing Individual Learning Units: Snapshots

Regardless of the format—seminar, lessons-learned session, mentoring relationship, sabbatical, site visit, independent research—a few basic guidelines, described in this section, expedite and invigorate design of individual events.

Relate the Activity to an Educational Strategy

Be clear on how a particular learning activity supports at least one of the firm's educational strategies. If you were Lukmire in year 3 of its plan (see Chapter 2), you would know that you should be designing either a Saturday workshop or a site visit. If you were FreemanWhite, your event could take any form, but it would have to do at least one of the following:

> Further employees' job performance.

> Stimulate cross-pollination among the firm's markets and/or services and/or organizational tenets.

> Strengthen the profession as a whole.

Identify and Support an Appropriate Expert

The expert can be from inside or outside the firm; a trainer, coach, or mentor; an advisor or resource. Command of content is essential, and so is ability to perform in the facilitator role. Some experts are terrific in classroom situations, but impatient in mentoring relationships. Some are acclaimed technical experts who should serve only as resources for independent research assignments. For an activity to be successful, be sure to:

> *Vet the expert,* in terms of technical know-how and knowledge-sharing effectiveness.

> *Support the expert*: Coach the people who will train, coach, and mentor others.

> *Prepare the expert for evaluations* of his or her performance. Professionals are accustomed to

Tip

Registered Providers of AIA's Continuing Education System have access to the *CES Provider Manual,* which bubbles with great information and ideas for the design of learning programs. The annual Provider fee for AIA architecture firms is so modest that the manual alone is worth every penny.

In Depth: Promoting Creativity

Cooper Roberts Simonsen Architects (CRSA) is a 33-person architecture and planning firm in Salt Lake City, Utah, that values creativity. Design of CRSA's professional development program sparks creativity and reflects staff's interests. Many of the following ideas were suggested by staff:

▶ *Traveling scholarships*. CRSA conducts an annual Traveling Scholarship competition. Eligible employees apply for travel anywhere in the world for personal and professional growth. Applications may include self-directed trips, group tours, research programs, conferences/seminars, volunteer programs, and others. Each year, one applicant is selected. Upon return, the employee presents his or her experience to the staff, sharing pictures and information, and spreading enthusiasm for future traveling scholarships.

▶ *Essay contest*. Employees are asked to write essays that explore aspects of the architectural profession. Judging is based on relevance, the thought that went into the essay, and the quality of the writing, and winners receive cash prizes. Topics addressed by past winners include "Over-Emphasis on Computer Technology in Today's Architecture Education," "Gothic Architecture" (presented in poetic form), and "How the Spiral Jetty [constructed in the Great Salt Lake] Created Community."

▶ *Breakfast at Charlie's*. Organized by employees, these events occur on selected Friday mornings in the office on employees' own time. One of the organizers selects a topic, which is identified in the announcement. Each participant brings in a breakfast food to share. One session involved preparation of elevation drawings for a local business whose building had been damaged in a fire. More frequently, participants brainstorm and sketch ideas on such problems as improving the Beck Street Corridor as an entrance to Salt Lake City; creating a workspace to respond to a flexible office and changing technology; Xeriscaping ideas for the south Gateway District; designing a personal home theater for a small apartment, and a conference table for CRSA charrette/lunch/box lunch/meeting purposes.

▶ *Sketching*. To encourage and nurture drawing skills, one of the firm's staff members has converted her artistic talent and ability into "Sketching with Lee" sessions. Interested participants bring their sketchbooks and pencils to a lunchtime meeting. Lee takes staff through a sketching exercise, and provides assistance and encouragement as needed. Subjects have included buildings, details, and still lifes.

▶ *Lunchtime videos*. Organizers search out videos that provide an in-depth look at the creative efforts of other architects.

receiving "A's," so a lukewarm reception can be devastating.

In sum, experts need material resources and administrative support as they develop event content. Mostly, however, they need time. And they need to know where they should charge their hours and how they will be rewarded for sharing their expertise. The more effort experts contribute in terms of the Involvement Model, the greater support they need.

Develop Learning Objectives

Learning objectives shape the event and ensure its success. As simple statements that anticipate outcomes for a learning activity, learning objectives explain what the novice will gain as a result of the experience. In a training activity, the expert determines most of the objectives, but may be counseled by representatives of the proposed audience. In other knowledge-sharing modes, the novice participates in projecting results.

Learning objectives are most helpful in designing an educational event if they are phrased in terms of the audience. One of the best models for scripting objectives is the National Architectural Accreditation Board, cited earlier in this chapter as an excellent resource. In its review of architecture schools, NAAB looks at student performance criteria in terms of three levels of proficiency: awareness, understanding, and ability. At NAAB, *awareness* refers to familiarity with specific information, facts, definitions, rules, processes, concepts, or the like. *Understanding* suggests assimilation and a degree of comprehension. *Ability* means that one can translate information into action.

☑ **Key Point**

Remember these points when formulating learning objectives:

► A learning objective should begin with, "At the end of this program, participants will…"

► A verb phrase should be next: "…be aware of," "…understand," or "…be able to…"

► A specific outcome should complete the objective.

Program Planning and Design 105

Clarity about the anticipated level of proficiency following a learning event sheds light on event content and design. For example, at the end of a proposed seminar on sustainable design, will participants be expected to:

> ➤ *Be aware of* the principals of sustainable design and LEED rating?

> ➤ *Understand* key technical elements of sustainable design, and the architect's responsibility under LEED?

> ➤ *Be able to* integrate sustainability into projects appropriately?

Any one of these learning objectives provides more guidance than one that simply says, "This program presents fundamental elements of sustainable design and the LEED rating system."

Center on the Learner

The more seasoned the professional, the less tolerant he or she will be of didactic learning methods. Even at the training level, seminars and workshops need to engage participants just as coaching and mentoring processes do (Chapter 5 talks about techniques). When knowledge sharing is the goal, event design has to incorporate ways for stimulating retention, such as appealing to Multiple Intelligences. And some subjects, like budgeting, are best presented to people by leading them through the Involvement Model: *training*, to introduce budget elements and the firm's budget development and reporting processes; *coaching*, to allow practice through fee-setting and budget reporting tasks; and *mentoring*, to test knowledge as a new PM with support from an experienced principal in charge (PIC).

One way to be sure that a new educational initiative appeals to people is to involve representative participants in designing the activity. If sabbaticals are proposed, then a potential candidate might offer advice on how to structure the activity so that the outcome serves both the learner and the firm. If mentoring is desirable, then the creators should include people who could participate as either experts or novices.

Strive for Progressive Feedback

Professionals enjoy testing a new idea or aptitude as soon as they grasp it. Attending a workshop on lighting, being coached on presentation skills, researching health care trends, or brainstorming new approaches to client interface spark staff contribution…maybe: If the time between their learning activity and their ability to act on it stretches too long, they will have difficulty assimilating what they have learned; they may even become frustrated.

Learning events can be designed to include the participants' own practice activities. Information-intensive workshops and seminars can start and end with a quiz that immediately reinforces the program's content and the participants' accomplishments. Research projects and individual learning initiatives can include progress reports and personal action plans. Competitions, critiques, and expert reviews can be built into many educational activities to satisfy the urge of participants to raise their own performance bar. Immediate feedback is one of the primary reasons that fans of interactive software enjoy the format.

Program Planning and Design

Be Fanatical about Health, Safety, and Welfare

Being current on health, safety, and welfare (HSW) matters is critical to design professionals. To serve the public effectively, firms must offer events that address emerging issues and reinforce existing HSW standards. Increasingly, design firms turn to outside organizations to import continuing education sessions to the firm, and/or to contribute to the design of the firm's proprietary vehicles. No matter who the provider of an HSW activity is, firms must assure that any event that claims to address HSW matters does so.

Design with an Eye to Evaluation and Change

The most elegantly crafted learning event is only temporary. Participants will recommend changes. Session leaders will test the degree to which their learning objectives were met, and adjust their methods accordingly. And, of course, content presented in the event will become obsolete. For good and for ill, professional practice is volatile, and learning events and knowledge-building approaches must adapt. As an educational event is being designed, so should a detailed evaluation format for it.

Do a Beta Test

Everyone benefits from a run-through prior to rolling out a continuing education initiative. The expert benefits from feedback on content, materials, techniques, and presentation style. The beta audience enjoys helping to refine a new learning initiative. Potential novices benefit from a more effective event. And the firm benefits from better quality.

Document

Designing effective learning events is an investment. Learning objectives, outlines, handouts, media, and evaluation forms should be documented, as should the cost of human and material resources for design and implementation. Evaluation results should include feedback on:

> How the event was received by participants.

> How their new knowledge was demonstrated in practice.

> How the event actually supported the firm's educational strategy.

The following chapters focus more closely on three knowledge-sharing formats that design firms favor in proprietary professional development programs: curricula, lessons-learned sessions, and mentoring relationships. But first, a plug for individual learning initiatives, which inspire all design professionals, mavericks among them.

Mavericks and Sole Proprietors

Mavericks and sole proprietors don't have much choice: Their professional development relies on self-directed learning and individual initiatives. But that's not a disadvantage. To support designers' creativity and hunger for knowledge, even large firms, awash in resources and rich in continuing education programs, promote a cowboy attitude about professional development. OWP/P, a Chicago multidisciplined firm, envisions an office environment in which learning is so powerful that the firm has little need for mandates and processes; Gensler, HOK, and NBBJ encourage and support staff to pursue their own interests.

When a corporation makes professional development a criterion for performance appraisal, facilities experts, who are in an essentially different business from everyone else, must expend a little more effort to comply. Holding licenses in multiple states doesn't make things any easier.

Insider Kenneth R. Stebbins, AIA: Planning to Learn

SUPERVALU is the largest food wholesale company in the United States. PLANMARK is its architectural/engineering arm, and Kenneth R. Stebbins, AIA, is vice president and director of Professional Services of the PLANMARK-Design Services Group.

In my role as director of Professional Services at PLANMARK, designing retail supermarkets and food distribution centers throughout the United States, I am currently registered in 41 states. 24 of those states have continuing education requirements, each with its own set of regulations. It has become a major effort to make sure that I am current with each state's requirements, and aware of changes occurring with the requirements of the other 17 states relative to continuing education regulations that may be pending.

PLANMARK and SUPERVALU are strong advocates of continuing education for all employees. My staff and I are expected to better ourselves from year to year, and continuing education activities factor in our annual performance reviews and personal development plans. PLANMARK supports this expectation by paying virtually all costs related to continuing education activities.

I am encouraged to participate in professional organizations. I sometimes attend conventions sponsored by the Food Marketing Institute and by Store Planning, Equipment and Construction Services (SPECS), but primarily I concentrate on AIA programs, national and state, trying to attend yearly. At last year's AIAMinnesota conference, I was intrigued by a presentation on wayfinding that addressed proper signage and visual references for users (store customers, in my case). By serving on AIA committees I developed leadership skills that have helped me succeed as director at PLANMARK.

I pursue other opportunities, including in-house vendor presentations, company training programs, and professional publications. Some journals regularly include articles that can be submitted for AIA/CES credit upon taking a short quiz. Also, many states offer online training courses that architects can take for continuing education credits. This option makes it easy for professionals like me to study at our own pace.

Program Planning and Design

Since PLANMARK works within a very limited range of building types, I look for ways to be informed of what is happening within the profession and in areas beyond our expertise. I am a magazine "junkie" and subscribe to many publications, such as *Architectural Record, Architecture, Engineering News Record, Wood Design & Building,* and *Design Solutions.* A magazine like *ID* covers a range of design issues, from graphics to products to automobiles to buildings to the built environment in general. I see how the design process is used in wide applications, touching so much of what we come into contact with every day.

Design and the development of concepts and ideas are key parts of what architects do. But equally important are the technical and business sides of architecture. I always find something valuable, refreshing, or intriguing from attending conferences and seminars, and from reading. I know that to set a good example for our employees and to continue to grow in my career, "planning to learn" is as important as learning to plan. Continuing education is the key to staying at the forefront of the profession.

The AIA, its chapters, and other professional associations are primary learning resources for mavericks and sole proprietors, as are technical and professional publications. Networking with colleagues and consultants generates more possibilities, and is good for business development, too. Just as small offices will sometimes team up to pursue a commission, so they muster resources to attract vendors and other external providers, or to develop joint events. For-profit training organizations offer seminars on a retail basis across the country, where mavericks enjoy the opportunity to meet new people as they gain new ideas.

Learning opportunities are everywhere. Architects accrue valuable insights and information when they participate in programs and on committees sponsored by their clients' professional organizations. Serving on community boards and task forces connects them more closely with public concerns and issues. Simple volunteer work—whether for an organization linked to the design professions or for one that reflects a personal interest—almost always benefits practice, directly or indirectly.

Teaching is a natural development initiative for architects, as other mavericks point out in later chapters, and volunteering at a university on a committee or special initiative is another option to stay close to emerging theory and young architects. Writing—books, articles, letters to the editor, stories, poetry—stimulates inventive minds in a distinctly personal way. And research, self-initiated or funded by a grant or foundation, can transform people's work.

Personal learning plans for mavericks and sole proprietors should blend formal and informal processes, individual and collegial activities, technical and theoretical subjects, along with spontaneous practice elements of observation and experimentation that remain the most natural and enjoyable learning modes for most designers. To create your personal plan, start a file and a calendar for charting the next 18 months of knowledge building. Identify requirements and time frames that you must meet to maintain your licenses and memberships, and include any other "must do's." Note a few other areas that you think you should pursue, and allow for flexibility. After all, what's the point of being a maverick if you can't be spontaneous?

Here are some ideas:

> Plan to attend at least one professional conference or seminar each quarter to refresh your command of health, safety, and welfare.

> For a committee or board on which you currently serve, identify two things you have learned that pertain to your professional work. How have you applied them to practice? Iden-

tify two more things you could learn about as you participate with this group.

➤ What volunteer work do you, or could you, perform to gain new insights to:

◆ People for whom you design places or spaces?

◆ Organizational or management approaches?

◆ Effective leadership or communication practices?

➤ Form a learning alliance with two other professionals, one of them a consultant or contractor. Share knowledge. Attend a professional seminar together every six months. Pool resources to invite an expert to conduct a learning event at one of your offices.

➤ Read a biography about someone you admire. What attitudes or approaches are worth emulating?

➤ Plan a study tour. Identify a style, location, building type, designer, setting, material, or place that you'd like to know more about, and outline learning objectives for yourself.

Curriculum 5

For good and for ill, the institution of seminars and formal classes is the first deliberate knowledge-sharing venture that most firms undertake. A common practice in the corporate world, an in-house university can be an efficient, reassuring, and satisfying format for transferring information and skills from experts to novices. It is efficient, because the experts who invest time in developing and presenting courses share their knowledge with numbers of staff at a time. It is reassuring, because an array of best practices is institutionalized through a familiar process. It is satisfying, because it stimulates continuous improvement in both expert and novice.

Alas, ill effects can be felt if establishing a curriculum is all that a firm does to advance knowledge. Architects have historically preferred learning within the context of projects, and learning activities limited to the basic level of the Involvement Model can seem remote from projects and clients, even inside a design firm. Professionals, who are accustomed to exploring independently and reflecting on their own experiences, can feel stifled by learning that is heavily weighted to classroom style. Of course, this latter point may be one of the reasons that a firm rushes to use a curriculum: It's a surefire way to institutionalize standards and practices.

As long as it is not the only way that a firm tries to build knowledge, a thoughtfully planned curriculum offers many benefits to the firm and its members. It can:

➤ Reinforce the firm's culture.

➤ Promote consistent project delivery and administrative practices.

➤ Spur communication and respect among members.

➤ Expedite the introduction of new systems and approaches.

➤ Adapt easily to accommodate innovation.

➤ Honor and promote in-house expertise.

➤ Provide access to outside experts.

➤ Support and encourage professional registrations, certifications, and memberships.

To reap such benefits, design firms must make the best use of educational resources. Firms typically want their curricula to include courses on professional, technical, business, and interpersonal subjects. Within each subject, they desire courses for an array of technical, administrative, and managerial employees. And they want to reach all staff in an office in which professionals are likely to have from 0 to 50 years' experience. Given these expectations, firms are wise to husband their resources, starting small and setting priorities.

Curriculum Design

Starting small does not mean designing one course at a time; nor does it mean offering a cluster of programs that reflect the latest firm crisis or the principal's greatest passion. Whether the curriculum is modest or sophisticated, many of the basic guidelines from Chapter 4, as well as the eight defined here expressly for curriculum development, are definite "do's."

Base Programs on the Firm's Strategy

A meaningful curriculum relates directly to the firm's current situation and/or future. In the early stages of curriculum development, FreemanWhite looked to the future. FWI decided to focus on its strategic goal for excellent client service, so most initial offerings centered on enhancement of project management skills. Over time, the firm's academy evolved to meet the newer strategic vision described in Chapter 2.

As Figure 5.1 indicates, in recent years FWI's in-house academy has matured to serve every staff member. Every course in the curriculum relates to at least one of the firm's six goals, which are listed in the top right corner of the chart. Every time someone registers for a seminar on the firm's intranet, the firm's goals are reinforced and related to learning.

One of Gresham, Smith and Partners' recent annual training plans addressed both strategic and immediate goals through five curricular initiatives:

> ▶ The first, Supervisory Training, was aimed at improving staff retention; it included an eight-hour basics course on human resource issues and interpersonal skills, supplemented with elective seminars.

> ▶ The second, Project Management Training, was a 12-hour series to reinforce the firm's branded approach to project management.

Tip

The International Association for Continuing Education and Training (IACET) is an excellent source of information about the development of training programs, especially those that comply with the recognized Continuing Education Unit (CEU) designation.

CORE and ENRICHMENT Courses		Learning Objective	Load	HSW	Firm's Strategic Goals					
Course Number (Core or Enrich.)			Course Time	Y=YES	The FreemanWhite Experience	Innovative Solutions	Measurable Results	Strengthen Credibility	Work Smart	Grow Smart
C	Or-1 — Orientation - General	To learn firm information in relation to goals, policies and procedures.	1.50		■				■	■
C	M-2 — Client Development and Maintenance	To understand the nature and upkeep of a business relationship.	2.00		■			■	■	
C	M-3 — Consultant Contracts, Coordination, and Management	Learn to manage working arrangements between architect & consultant.	2.00		■	■		■	■	
E	M-3a — Risk for Managers	Enhance understanding of legal risks involved in the design industry.	3.00	Y	■	■		■	■	■
E	M-7 — Leadership	Advance leadership skills and qualities.	2.00		■	■	■		■	■
C	H-1 — Employment Practices Training for Managers	Learn new laws, relations, and general employment practices.	3.00		■			■	■	■
C	S-13 — Computer Simulation	Learn basic principals of simulation and how it can help your project.	2.00		■	■	■		■	
C	T-1a — Code - Research and Process	Learn how to prepare a code analysis, and Principles of Life Safety	1.50	Y	■	■			■	
E	T-4a — Specifications - Division 1: General Conditions	Understand the contractual requirements of specifications.	1.00	Y	■	■		■	■	
E	T-10 — The International Building Code	Learn major features of the new code.	2.00	Y	■	■			■	
C	T-12 — Principals of Document Coordination	The basics of interdisciplinary checking and drawing.	2.00		■			■	■	
E	T-20 — PM Training Summary & Review	Review project manager summary and allow for questions and follow-up.	3.00		■	■			■	
E	I-1 — IDP/ARE Open Discussion	Participants should get a general overview of IDP and ARE requirements.	2.00		■				■	■
C	A-1 — Understanding the Field of Architecture	Introductory course regarding the design and construction trades.	1.50		■	■		■	■	■
E	O-2 — Process mapping	FWI's process of simulation used in the Healthcare Consulting services.	1.50		■	■	■			
E	O-10 — Interactive Marketing & Research	Learn how marketing research helps FWI better understand its clients.	1.50		■	■		■	■	
E	O-13 — Trends in Healthcare Design	A critical look at healthcare design and how it pertains to FW.	1.50		■	■		■	■	
E	V-25 — Medical Gas/NFPA 99 Update	Review of medical gas requirements in critical areas and NFPA 99 updates.	1.50	Y	■	■		■	■	

Figure 5.1 Sample of courses with related strategic goals from the FreemanWhite Academy.

➤ Technical/Professional Training, which covered many topics and skills, addressed design and document quality.

➤ To improve staff productivity, Information Technology Training included CADD, graphics, and office automation.

➤ Employee Orientation was offered twice a month to inform new staff about the firm's history, markets, tools and resources, as well as its proprietary Career Development System.

Center on the Learner

Center on the learner means designing for the roles that people fill. A curriculum should be designed with an eye to individual roles and performance measurements. An in-house curriculum must reflect what people need, want to know, and can use immediately. If participants can't test, apply, or observe what they have learned, their enthusiasm for that knowledge erodes. If they are repeatedly unable to connect learning to their work, they may feel disenfranchised by the firm's learning program, or, worse yet, cynical about it.

NBBJ offers courses on professional and personal matters to engage all employees. Technical subjects include codes, specifications, detailing, structures, and presentation technology. Interior design, architectural design, and project delivery address broader issues. Seminars in business, liability, presentation skills, and office technology promote management and administrative performance. Personal development and psychology speak directly to people's individual performance. The curriculum is planned to appeal to all staff.

But sometimes appeal isn't enough. Not long after the FreemanWhite Academy was in place, the firm's leadership realized that staff members were not as diligent about tapping into the academy as had been envisioned. Customizing the curriculum to relate directly to the positions that people held currently, and aspired to in the future, immediately commanded staff attention. When the firm went a step further and linked professional development to performance appraisals and promotions, the academy and the firm's practice were fully integrated. Today, as shown in Figure 5.1, FWI's program includes a customized core curriculum for all positions in the firm: managing principals, administrative assistants, project managers, interns, registered architects and engineers, sustainability experts, and registered nurses among them. In the figure, the letters C and E in the first column stand for Core and Enrichment courses, respectively. In the second column, the letter prefix of each course number identifies the general topic:

A for Administrative
H for Human Resources
I for Intern
M for Managerial
O for Orientation
S for Software
T for Technical
V for Vendor Products
O for Other

Address Complex Topics through Series

Many practice topics cannot be wrapped up in 60 to 90 minutes. For example, project manager training, which appears in many firms' curricula, encompasses so many knowledge areas and skill sets that it almost always is addressed through a series of workshops. Whether the PM series is sequential or presented as a collection of classes in no particular order, it is likely to include topics as varied as the following:

Project planning

Schedules

Budgets

Roles and responsibilities

Quality control

Construction administration

Extra services

Project closeout

Invoices and collection

Contracts

Negotiations

Ethics

Managing staff

Delegation

Communications

Marketing

Managing consultants

Managing client expectations

Team building

Leadership

A series this extensive can be delivered through several daylong retreats or in 8 to 12 sessions of 90 minutes. It can be organized into a core cluster of classes offered exclusively to PM candidates, with other sessions open to all managers. Some sessions might be required, with others either elective or required at specific points in a PM's development. In any case, serial courses require a flexible curriculum.

Identify and Support Experts

The expert pool for design firms is broad: senior staff and in-house gurus, outside experts in everything from fire protection to contracts; manufacturers and vendors; business and marketing consultants; educators and researchers; clients and public-sector representatives; builders and subconsultants. Though many of these experts may be experienced speakers and teachers, the firm should have and follow its own guidelines and standards to make sure that the efforts of trainers, coaches, and mentors are fruitful for the firm.

After the firm has identified topics that reinforce its long-range plan, and people who need exposure to the topics, it looks for appropriate experts to share their knowledge. HOK turns to members of the firm who are current on AIA/CES guidelines, are involved with colleges and universities in teaching or board roles, and have taken workshops on teaching or facilitation skills within three years. At Gresham, Smith, and Partners, every employee who instructs a course that will be offered firmwide must attend the firm's Train-the-Trainer class. If the employee has never taught at the firm, he or she may also observe or co-teach a class in preparation for the first solo venture. Systems like this enable a course to be led effectively by multiple experts.

Processes should be developed to:

> ► Identify experts who are qualified to address subject matter.

> ► Provide them with either a course outline or with a format for their use in preparing content.

> ► Introduce them to effective teaching/learning techniques, as discussed in the "Course Design" section, later in this chapter.

> Provide individual coaching and/or the opportunity for observation and practice.

> Provide feedback and opportunity for improvement.

The constraints inherent in a seminar format demand that even the most renowned technical specialist be conscious of teaching and learning processes. Conducting a course is not the same as presenting the firm's qualifications to a prospective client or a design solution to an existing one, although experience in any venue is likely to enhance one's performance in the others.

Tap Outside Providers

Proprietary, custom-designed courses should dominate the curricula of firms that want to reap the benefits described in Chapter 1, but excellent generic programs on topics from marketing to specifications are available from outside organizations and can be woven into the firm's proprietary program.

Many product suppliers and manufacturers offer solid educational seminars to design firms. Their sessions not only provide valuable information about building materials, and systems, but also address health, safety, and welfare matters that respond to architects' state licensing requirements. The AIA can be a helpful resource in this regard, because vendors that are registered providers of the AIA's Continuing Education System must meet AIA standards for program design and objectivity. The offerings of almost a thousand AIA Stakeholder Providers are vetted through mandatory course registration processes and random audits.

Some engineers, specialist consultants, builders, subcontractors, and even other architects conduct

Key Point

When designing a curriculum for design firms, use these eight "do's" as guidelines:

1. Base programs on the firm's strategy.
2. Center on learners' roles.
3. Address complex topics through series.
4. Identify and support experts.
5. Tap outside providers.
6. Include distance learning opportunities.
7. Decide on a basic module.
8. Avoid hubris.

educational workshops and classes for design firms. Attorneys, accountants, management and marketing consultants, and continuing education specialists are additional sources of workshops that can be incorporated into a firm's curriculum. Industry-related publishing and training companies, such as Professional Services Management Journal (PSMJ) Resources and Zweig White & Associates, Inc., are willing to deliver their seminars at design firm offices. Many of these organizations will modify or design courses to respond to a firm's specific needs. In some cases even academics will come to a firm. The Boston Architectural Center's seminar program, the Campus of Campuses, brings continuing education programs into design firms in the Boston and Cambridge areas.

A firm must demand the same of outsiders as of internal experts. To incorporate external continuing education events like these into its curriculum, a firm should assess seminar content and quality, preview the presenter's credentials, understand how information in the session will translate into practice, and schedule sessions in advance. To aid in this review process, members of the firm may be able to observe outside providers at conventions and/or to review audio- or videotapes.

With or without previous exposure, both the firm and the external provider need information from each other. A firm should give to the outside provider:

> ► At least six months' notice.

> ► A written request for qualifications that spells out the expectations on both sides. For example, the tradition of vendor-supplied lunches at product sales presentations is so prevalent that a

firm might mistakenly assume that external providers always contribute food platters, as well as education. In reality, that great vendor training program may come with an honorarium invoice, rather than chicken caesar salads.

- Information about logistics (schedule and site) and attendees (including number of attendees, their roles in the firm, years of experience).

- A one-page fact sheet about the firm, including staff composition, markets, services, approach to professional development, and any other information that would help an outsider prepare a session tailored to the audience.

- Samples of any of the firm's tools or systems that should be reinforced during the external provider's session.

The provider should give to the firm:

- A completed qualifications outline or application form.

- A brief outline of seminar content.

- A list of equipment and facility needs.

- Brief biographies of the presenters.

- References.

Include Distance Learning Opportunities

One of the advantages of a curriculum format is the ease with which it accommodates learning from a distance. Architects who work part-time, or travel frequently to serve out-of-state clients, or practice at offices remote from a firm's home base can access their firm's proprietary program through the Internet or CD-ROMs, by synchronous teleconferencing, by video- or audiotape. Seminar handouts, combined with an expert's written notes or taped presentation, make an effective workbook. And the addition of pre-tests and post-tests, worksheets, "homework" assignments, and the like result in a learning approach that is very appealing to some professionals.

Flexibility and easy access are advantages of distance learning formats. And ability of "students" to retain and apply information and ideas can be improved through a medium that they control. As an expert in quality control, Philip W. Kabza, AIA, CSI, CCS, observed that young designers needed to be more facile in construction documentation and specification. But it seemed that information presented in seminars wasn't always integrated into actual practice. To close that gap, Kabza decided to use the Internet to serve people byte-sized learning nuggets, each day (see Figure 5.2). The process sometimes required them to perform a little research, but it enabled them to do so at their convenience.

Using a program from the Construction Specifications Institute (CSI) as a base, Kabza developed multiple-choice questions and identified the appropriate source for answers to each of them. Meting the questions out as 15-minute learning segments allowed for the introduction of a new question, and review of a previous one, in time frames that respected busy schedules.

"CDT One Day at a Time!" became an award-winner, and SpecGuy an easily accessible expert on document technology, because the material was expressly adapted for Internet use. The education needs of the distance learner determine content and form. A process for engaging learners through quizzes and pre/post-tests raises the likelihood that they

From: CDT@SpecGuy.com

Date: Thu, Oct 3, 2002, 10:23 PM

To: <jrvalence@blackridge.com>

Subject: CDT One Day at a Time!

CDT One Day at a Time! No. 04

CDT One Day at a Time! is your daily reminder to keep working at mastering the content of the CSI Manual of Practice.

Your CDT Question of the Day is:

The general clauses that establish how the project is to be administered are known as:

a. Conditions of the Contract

b. General Conditions

c. Supplementary Conditions

d. Addenda

Review:

MOP Fundamentals and Formats Chapter 030

Yesterday's Question:

When is the CSI/CSC UniFormat used?

a. When a project is in the design development stage.

b. In the planning stage of a project.

c. In the post-construction phase of a project.

d. To organize information by materials and methods.

e. In the schematic design phase of a project.

Yesterday's Review:

MOP Fundamentals and Formats Chapters 020 and 180

Yesterday's Answer:

e. In the schematic design phase of a project. UniFormat is particularly useful for filing information, organizing preliminary project descriptions, and filing detail drawings.

CDT One Day at a Time! is ©Copyright 2001-2002 SpecGuy

Mail to: CDT@SpecGuy.com

www.SpecGuy.com

Figure 5.2 Online learning program. © 2001 SpecGuy. All rights reserved.

will retain what they have read, seen, and heard. And proprietary online educational programs can be designed for easy modification, so that the firm benefits quickly from improvements.

As is the case for traditional seminars, distance learning programs are available from external experts, online and on CD-ROMs. In addition to a preview of their materials, distance educators should provide an explanation of their process and time frame for updating material, their system for orientation and technical support, and their method for soliciting and responding to performance feedback from participants.

Decide on a Basic Module

The development of a standard module simplifies and expedites the design and implementation of a collective curriculum and its individual pieces. Ninety minutes is the favored module-segment length for design firms, and noontime the preferred time slot, for practical and philosophical reasons. Practically, participants and instructors find that scheduling time over lunch is easiest for them during busy workdays, and more respectful of their personal lives. Philosophically, the firm invests in a program, the professional invests time, and both perceive a mutual commitment to professional development.

A 60-minute module, especially if lunch is involved, is inadequate for most subjects. Health, safety, welfare matters usually demand more time. And, with an extra half-hour, an expert can address one topic in depth, and participants can interact with the material through hands-on demonstration, case study, critique, and the like. For a professional audience, such direct involvement by learners facilitates application to practice.

The basic module should also be flexible enough to accommodate wide-ranging topics, presentation techniques, learning styles, and internal and external providers. Refer back to Figure 5.1, which shows that the FreemanWhite sample sessions include those that run from 1.5 to 3 hours, with 90- and 120-minute events predominating.

Avoid Hubris

The construction of an in-house university is a major undertaking, and, once a firm has launched its curriculum, the creators may be resistant to modifications. For that reason, a requirement for revision should be built into the program from the outset. Courses should be refreshed and redesigned to reflect new trends and feedback from participants. Instructors should rotate, and some sessions should be transitioned to other experts. Even the most passionate advocators must remember two things: the in-house university is not a real university, and tenure is inappropriate.

Course Design

In designing a course, the expert balances technical content and delivery methods, just as he or she would in making a presentation to a client.

Insider Michael D. Perry, Honorary AIA:
Developing a Continuing Education Course for Architects

A veteran of the roofing industry, Mike Perry noticed an increasing demand for environmentally sensitive construction. He also respected architects' caution about unfamiliar construction methods. Determining that the most effective way to introduce green roofing technology would be by educating professionals, Perry set out to design a seminar for architects. Along the way, he educated himself so effectively that he changed career focus and is now president of Building Logics, Inc., providers of environmentally friendly building products, and specialists in green roofing technology and information. Here he describes his experience in developing his first "green" program for architects.

My first step was to convince myself that green roofing alternatives were available and as good as, or better than, existing practices. Since the technology was not available in the United States, I traveled to Europe where green technology had been employed for decades. Touring labs, factories, construction sites, and facilities, I became convinced of the viability and superior performance of an eco-roof system to replace naturally vegetated areas destroyed by construction of buildings and other nonpervious surfaces. Now my mission was to address architects' learning curve about vegetated systems.

Before joining a roofing company 17 years earlier, I had studied architecture and worked in the profession, so I understood the learning style preferred by my target audience. Visualization is one of an architect's best abilities, and architects must also touch, feel, see, smell (and, in some cases, taste) a new product before they will consider using it for a project. My education program was designed to reflect these learning preferences.

Graphic material opened the dialogue with my audience and created an awareness of the issues that could be corrected with the implementation of this new approach. Various examples of poor practices in the construction industry were identified, photographed, and documented to illustrate the need.

To engage the architect, I decided to use a pretest, either written or spoken. This test would allow my audience to realize what they did not know and to recognize needs for environmentally sensitive construction. It also set the stage for the rest of the program.

At this point, I explained the technology's history, much of which I had gained from my European research, and discussed green roofing successes and failures during its development. Moving into the current technology age, I showed photographs of the actual manufacturing process of the system's various components. In green roofing, each component must work in unison with the others, so I decided to spend several minutes identifying the critical elements of each component and discussing issues related to each.

To ensure audience participation and retention, I incorporated samples into this part of the course. Architects handled components to help them remember the importance of each element. Hearing me say that a membrane would stretch would be one thing, but stretching it themselves would mean that participants would never forget the information. This kind of hands-on involvement was planned throughout the program.

After the audience had developed a good understanding of the need for the technology, its history, and the product elements, I illustrated the total system through photographs, articles, and system mock-ups. Then I presented ecological and practical benefits of a green roof in terms of overall value. Matching the level of technical information to the audience, I used scientific evidence with reports, charts, and graphs. While no one would expect me to be to be a scientist, a botanist, a landscape architect, or a chemist, I was prepared to talk technically to well-informed people.

At the conclusion I summarized all key points, telling people again what I had already told them. An effective method of getting my points across in other presentations, I knew repetition would be important for this topic, too.

After planning the presentation, I revisited it, making sure that I had included sufficient time for audience participation, questions, and answers, and that I had incorporated questions to pose to the attendees, inviting them to share their personal knowledge and experiences of the subject matter with each other.

The programs have been well received across the United States, and I enjoy developing and presenting them, believing that we must all become stewards of the world in which we live.

Perry began with a clear purpose and performed research necessary for conveying his information and ideas to an audience. He scripted a course that reflected the ways his audience likes to learn and he bookended his material with an introduction and a summary.

Most important, participants were actively engaged in meaningful activities that did not rely on Q&A exchange. For design professionals, at least one-third of any session should be planned for direct engagement through demonstrations and hands-on experience, case study discussion, juries, model-making, small group assignments, and the like. Tests and quizzes, checklists, workbooks, and software allow individuals to work on their own at moments during the course. A combination of both collegial and independent involvement is effective for professionals, which is one of the reasons that many design firms favor a 90-minute session. Handouts that can be reviewed following the course help effect transition to practice, as well as serve as a reference during the session. And any feedback mechanism—tests, juries, software cues, observation by an expert, practice with a coach—expedites learning.

To help experts develop courses, the firm can request completion of a course or seminar proposal, like that in Figure 5.3. The form guides the person completing it to outline the course. First the expert relates the course to a strategic goal and composes learning objectives to keep the course focused. Then the applicant is asked to identify each key point with accompanying presentation techniques and processes for audience participation.

Question 4 reminds the expert to design course material for application to professional practice. Some sessions may be designed with a follow-up coaching effort or a "homework" assignment. Question 5 raises the instructor's consciousness of learning through teaching. The query about health, safety, and welfare (HSW) at the top of the form is important, so that programs addressing such matters can be assured to meet current licensing criteria.

A Course Submission Form, developed by the Interior Design Continuing Education Council represents a more detailed format, and can be accessed through the International Interior Design Association website www.iida.org. Like Figure 5.3, it can be modified for use by in-house experts, manufacturers who provide lunch-and-learn sessions, and for-profit training companies proposing to deliver workshops to the firm. If clients are invited to serve as

Key Point

When designing an individual course, use these "do's" as guidelines:

1. Link to firm's strategy.
2. Write learning objectives.
3. Reserve one-third of the session for engagement.
4. Bookend with introduction and summary.
5. Develop a script.
6. Use multiple media.
7. Rehearse.
8. Document.
9. Evaluate.

Seminar Proposal

Date: _____

Subject: _____   Instructor: _____

Length of seminar: _____   HSW? _____

Title: _____

1. Identify the strategic goal(s) that this seminar supports.

   ▶

   ▶

2. Identify the learning objectives for this seminar, starting each with "Be aware of," "Understand," or "Be able to." At the end of this seminar participants will:

   ▶

   ▶

   ▶

3. Outline the seminar content by section using the chart shown, including your key points, the presentation techniques you will use, and the ways that participants will actively engage with your information and concepts during the seminar. Engagement might include pre-tests and post-tests, practice and hands-on demonstration, small group discussions, personal action plan development, and so on.

Content/ Key Points	Presentation Methods/ Media	Participant Involvement

4. Identify opportunities participants will have to apply their new learning after they have completed the seminar.

   ▶

5. Explain how you will benefit from developing and/or presenting this seminar.

   ▶

Figure 5.3 Seminar proposal.

Curriculum

experts, they receive the same preparation and support as in-house instructors.

Of course, keeping competitive edge in mind, as a firm develops its particular seminar proposal processes, it incorporates criteria that reflect the firm's unique culture. For example, according to the "NBBJ Continuing Education Program" published by the firm's Columbus, Ohio, office, courses must do at least one of four things. A course must:

> "Add to the architect's toolkit, allowing us to develop better people, processes, and products for our clients.

> Help our office keep abreast of the latest advances in technology that may affect or improve our office functions and design quality.

> Ensure that information that exists in our office is disseminated throughout the office, involving all aspects of our business from architecture to business to liability to operations.

> Allow us to be more proactive in avoiding architectural trouble spots and common problems."

All courses should be rehearsed and documented, as mentioned in Chapter 4. At Gresham, Smith, every firmwide course is reviewed by a focus group and beta-tested before a mock audience. Gensler is similarly formal about training initiatives. Although the firm encourages casual coaching and mentoring relationships within individual offices, globally, Gensler rolls out classes taught by experts in each office from a developed curriculum. Two to three structured classes are offered per quarter, supplemented with outside speakers and vendors.

In any firm, experts should be reminded that their programs will be evaluated by participants and that instructors will receive the results. As a firm builds its offerings, some sessions will probably be designated as core courses, planned for consistency regardless of the expert providing them, and updated regularly to meet current trends. Others will come and go, as the firm's strategy and assessed learning needs and opportunities dictate. And any new course must be marketed to busy professionals who are very selective of where they invest their professional development time and effort.

Mavericks and Sole Proprietors

Although learning about specific subjects through seminars and courses is difficult for mavericks to map very far in advance, topics and providers on general subjects can be identified:

- ▶ Announcements of the annual and regional programs offered by professional associations are published months ahead.

- ▶ Niche training companies promote traveling seminars early and, typically, provide content outlines and information about format and materials.

- ▶ Distance learning providers publish catalogs of online courses, tapes, and CD-ROMs that can be incorporated into an annual professional development plan.

For many architects, teaching itself is one of the most powerful learning approaches they ever experience, particularly for growth of nontechnical skills.

Insider Frederick Noyes, FAIA: Teaching Is Learning

Frederick Noyes, FAIA, leads a small architectural firm and volunteers extensively at the Boston Architectural Center (BAC). A past chairman of the BAC board of directors and frequent studio critic and instructor, Noyes has found that teaching is learning. His observations apply to designers who are considering a leadership role in their firm's internal professional development program, as well as to mavericks who are weighing the benefits of part- or full-time teaching at a design school.

Why does a practitioner choose to teach part-time? In office life, a professional is likely dealing with the hard knocks of architecture as a business—confronting contracts, endless notes, codes, and money disputes. Also, many professionals, particularly young ones, aren't making as many substantive design decisions as they had hoped. This is not exactly Architecture, with a capital "A," that inspired one's original commitment to the field or that typified one's education. So where to reconnect with that spirit? Why teaching, of course.

Teaching benefits the practitioner in many ways.

- ► Teachers look at myriad buildings from students with myriad backgrounds and skills. Teachers must give articulate, constructive feedback, which forces them to consolidate thoughts and opinions and to hone communication skills. For a new teacher, these thoughts often have been sloshing around half-baked since school days.

- ► The range of approaches students try is usually broader than in practice. And a teacher cannot dismiss or neglect maverick students as easily as one might in practice, when the first responsibility is to the project. Hence, the teaching practitioner is forced to fully engage new or even bad ideas—which helps keep one's eyes wide open and receptive, even to one's own doodlings during the design process. Design is a curious mix of revision, experience, use of prototypes, and invention. It is difficult not to become stale, cycling back on thoughts or solutions from past projects. So keeping one's eyes fresh is a very significant benefit of teaching.

- ► Except for presenting projects at school, young practitioners have seldom led discussions or given direction or have had to express themselves succinctly or manage group dynamics. Teaching may be the first time a young practitioner has been in a real architectural leadership position. The experience is invaluable in the office, for making client presentations or leading project teams.

> ▶ Organizing a class, complete with the project description, schedules, expectations of the students, grades, counseling, student feedback, and so on, is a skill that a teacher must learn. Organizing an office project (or even an office) is a direct beneficiary.
>
> Teaching also benefits sole practitioners, in these areas:
>
> > ▶ *People contact.* For a member of a small office, contact with peers is an especially valuable aspect of teaching.
> >
> > ▶ *Scuttlebutt.* Exposure to the outside world is particularly difficult in a small office. Time for professional activities is limited, as employees wear many hats. Teaching keeps one abreast of events, helps one establish a reputation, and connects one with people and other offices.
>
> But teaching can also have detrimental results:
>
> > ▶ If teachers go into a classroom to counter boring office work, they can become intoxicated by the ego boost. Juries become human barbecues, where critics try to make points with each other, showing how smart they are or how broad their knowledge. The learner is in a cross-fire, perhaps subject to derogatory comments.
> >
> > ▶ Teachers are sometimes guilty of promoting the incomprehensible architectural jargon that pervades the profession.
> >
> > ▶ Teachers can begin to take themselves too seriously. School is school; ideas must be tested in the marketplace.
>
> Charlie Gwathmey, of Gwathmey Siegel and Associates, once told me that teaching was for the young and the old—a comment I found curiously incomprehensible at the time (he was my teacher, then in his thirties). It now makes more sense to me. Midcareer professionals, grappling with the difficulties of running an office, frequently give comments overburdened with the practical: code issues, cost concerns, number of parking spaces. But typical new teachers (as I was) are young, a few years out of school, just a couple of steps ahead of the students they teach, and eager to impart the architectural ideas from their own schooling. And older practitioners have mellowed and think about broader architectural issues.

Whether expert or novice, facilitator or learner, participation in formal courses and seminars shortens the learning curve for many skills and efficiently spreads information and ideas among professionals.

Coaching and Lessons Learned

6

Coaching may be the most powerful and least utilized form of internal knowledge building available to design firms.

Some organizations, often large firms like Gensler, craft specific coaching processes to help foster emerging talent and to ensure that people are valued as individuals. At Gensler, a coach has the relevant skills to help someone build a career and the commitment to doing so. Critic and advisor, the Gensler coach meets regularly with the learner, to discuss professional goals and set professional development strategies; the coach also advocates on behalf of the learner. One-on-one sponsorship relationships like Gensler's are effective for the individuals involved and for the firms that arrange them. Most firms, however, prefer to focus coaching on the enhancement of people's professional development, rather than on career development.

As depicted earlier, in Figure 4.5, coaching is the 50–50 expert–novice relationship sandwiched between training and mentoring. At this engagement level, the facilitator works side by side with the learner, observing the learner in action, setting up situations to test and improve the learner's abilities, supporting and guiding the learner to greater achievement. In design firms, these opportunities arise every day, in the form of projects. The relationship between team leader and team provides a natural coach–learner synergy. And the coach is able to develop professionally, too.

Note

One-on-one coaching relationships are described later in this chapter's "Mavericks and Sole Proprietors" section. The following section recommends a variation that is viable for most firms, regardless of size, and that applies coaching techniques broadly to projects.

Lessons Learned

Lessons learned is simply the deliberate act of building knowledge during the accomplishment of projects, under the watchful eye of the project manager. Professionals always learn tacitly through their work; lessons learned replaces tacit, individual learning with articulated, shared learning that extends throughout the team, and sometimes beyond.

Lessons learned benefits the firm in many ways. It:

➤ Intensifies quality awareness during project delivery.

➤ Provides immediate opportunity to improve client satisfaction.

➤ Serves as a proving ground for concepts introduced in a curriculum.

➤ Directly relates learning to practice.

➤ Invites coaches to be role models for knowledge building.

➤ Regularly channels fresh client and market research into the firm.

➤ Captures and extends senior staff know-how.

➤ Builds team attitude.

➤ Stimulates trust and delegation.

➤ Enhances communication.

➤ Weaves learning into a billable activity.

Lessons learned also has some advantages over other methods. It is more easily implemented than an in-house university and more widely accessible than mentoring. And in terms of the learning dynamic (refer back to Figure 2.2), lessons learned generates within each project a vortex of information and ideas from the firm's past experience and from its current team members, clients, and consultants. Once synthesized, this knowledge becomes part of the firm's institutional wisdom to be applied to future projects and to advance the firm's long-range vision.

Organizing a Project for Learning

A complete lessons-learned process begins with the *establishment of learning objectives* at the firm's in-house project kickoff. Some of these objectives might be shared with, and expanded by, the larger team, perhaps even with clients. But in-house objectives are at least as important as those broadly shared, because the in-house objectives reflect and support the firm's unique competitive attributes.

Project learning objectives cover many topics, and the NAAB language presented in Chapter 4 reflects just how comprehensive, or focused, project learning can be: "At the end of this project, team members will be aware of" or "understand" or "be able to . . ." introduces potential learning about matters related to design and construction, management and leadership, client service and marketing, facility types and markets, and the like. A firm might dramatically increase its value to clients if it decided that at the end of every project, team members would understand at least one new aspect of the client's business, or be aware of one new trend in the client's world.

Key Point

Lessons-learned elements include:

► Establishment of learning objectives
► Assignments to team members
► Sessions at project milestones
► Final session at project wrap-up
► Archival of key information

With objectives in place, the *team leader assigns each objective*, or some aspect of an objective, to team members for consideration as they work on the project. *At project milestones, team members share their observations* to date and seek input from their colleagues. The feedback is used to refine their charges for review at the next project milestone, as well as to bolster product and service quality. Team members also discuss things they are learning and need to investigate further, beyond the initial objectives.

At the conclusion of the project, a *final lessons-learned session* describes the results of all the learning objectives and identifies the unanticipated knowledge that accrued to the team in the course of the project. Whether or not other members of the firm are invited to the final session, a *record of key information* becomes part of the firm's knowledge base, readily available and easily accessed. Topics for further investigation can be addressed through either other project teams or special research efforts.

One Firm's Experience

At Reynolds, Smith and Hills, Inc. (RS&H), architects and engineers in Jacksonville, Florida, lessons learned is a popular process in the Commercial Group, which encompasses approximately 50 people within the office. The firm has adapted the process to suit its needs, and the process is not ironclad, but typically:

- ▶ The director of the group and the director of the office select a project. At least half the group members must have been involved in the project for it to be eligible for a lessons-learned session.

- ▶ Lessons learned is conducted after the final project closeout.

> Only members of the firm may attend the mandatory three-hour session, which is scheduled from 4:00 to 7:00 P.M. Pizza is served and time is charged to overhead.

> The project manager leads the process and sets the agenda, drawing on outlines of past sessions for ideas.

> Data about the project and team are compiled and presented, including the project's location, size, cost, delivery method, fee, number of drawings, services provided, and schedule, as well as the identity of the team members, client, user, developer, consultants, general contractor, subs, and the like.

> Notes are taken during the session, and afterwards they are distributed to team members, archived, and made available to other PMs.

> Conversations continue after the session, as people pursue best practices.

An agenda for an RS&H lessons learned generally covers at least seven topics:

1. *Marketing history:* How did the project come into the office?

2. *Proposal:* What did we promise (e.g., services, scope, budget, fee, schedule), and why? How did we perform on each promise?

3. *Project delivery:* What was the delivery method? For example, were we to prepare full bid documents in a traditional process, or permit documents for a developer, or design-build documents for a contractor?

4. *Design:* How did the design evolve? What were the "givens?" The parameters? The client's preconceived notions? What was the impact of value engineering?

5. *Documents:* What was learned about documentation? For example, was the level of detail different than anticipated? What does each discipline have to say about its own documentation effort?

6. *Construction administration:* What was learned?

7. *Final close-out:* What was learned?

© Reynolds, Smith & Hills, Inc.

As a communications tool, lessons learned contributes both to the people who participate in the process and to the firm at large.

Insiders Jim Hawkes, AIA, and Chung Rutter, AIA:
Lessons Learned for Team Building and Personal Growth
at Reynolds, Smith and Hills

In November 1998, John Bottaro, AIA, an RS&H principal responsible for the firm's Commercial Group, attended one of the AIA/CES's Firm Leadership Summits. During a case study session, in which I introduced lessons learned as a professional development tool, Bottaro was so intrigued that he adopted the concept immediately for his group. According to Bottaro, within a few years the process had positively affected profitability and design quality. According to two senior architects who joined RS&H subsequent to 1998, lessons learn has even more immediate benefits.

Jim Hawkes

When I started at Reynolds, Smith and Hills three years ago, I had a lot to learn. RS&H has an arsenal of project management resources and guidelines the likes of which I had never been exposed to before. Even the basic principle of building a multi-disciplined team was foreign to me. But of all the new things, "lessons learned" has proven the most valuable. One of the best outcomes is team building on the interpersonal level, across disciplines and within disciplines.

On the interpersonal level, a lessons-learned session is a forum to air complaints and to resolve problems in a controlled environment, where everyone can express their point of view. Outside the heat of the project, this session is often the first chance team members have to listen to each other on an issue. Resolving personal conflicts in this manner creates stronger person-to-person relationships, which are the foundation of a good team.

Coaching and Lessons Learned

The session encourages better understanding among disciplines. It is fascinating to observe how differently people perceive the cause of problems and coordination conflicts. Discussion helps team members to understand key issues and constraints that other disciplines face, and to do things that allow others to do their jobs effectively.

The process also builds teams within disciplines, allowing younger architects and engineers to see the bigger picture and truly grow from facing the challenges of a project. Senior professionals learn new things, too, and they also become more sensitive to their younger colleagues.

Lessons learned is one of RS&H's strongest team-building tools, helping us refine our working relationships, understand other disciplines, and grow as professionals.

Chung Rutter

The first time I heard the phrase "lessons learned," I was being recruited by Reynolds Smith. During the interview, I learned that the firm often utilizes post-project evaluation sessions, referred to as "lessons learned," as an opportunity for the entire project team (including principals and administrative assistants) to share project issues, successes, and ideas for proceeding with future projects. Notes from these sessions are distributed to the participants and to other project managers as planning guides for future, similar projects. The technique made a big impression on me and was one of the reasons I decided to join the firm.

One of my first PM assignments was a new 75,000-square-foot office/manufacturing facility. Although I had practiced for over 10 years, some aspects of the project were new to me, among them a developer client, build-to-suit delivery method, and tilt wall construction. The team was obviously new to me, too. I was immediately offered notes from a previous lessons-learned session concerning a similar project, and those notes proved invaluable as I established our project management plan.

Following project close-out, my team held our own lessons-learned session. Afterwards a few younger associates mentioned that they found the session very eye-opening and that they had a better awareness of what is "black, white, and gray" as a result. The session proved to be informative for me, too, because I became aware of marketing issues and existing client relationships that explained some of our client's decisions.

On my first project for RS&H, I twice benefited professionally from lessons learned, once through someone else's notes from a previous session, and a second time through my own session.

Variations on Lessons Learned

Lessons-learned initiatives, reflecting each firm's culture and current priorities, vary in form, frequency, and purpose. HOK project managers have the option of instigating state-of-the-project assessment sessions at the end of each phase, engaging the entire team—including clients, consultants, and contractor—in a discussion about the project's progress. Information resides with the team for application to the remainder of the project and for individuals' personal growth.

San Diego, California, firm Carrier Johnson uses a version of lessons learned that prompts project architects to lead monthly site walks during construction, so that the team can observe what worked, what didn't, and how problems were solved. On fast-track projects that overlap design and construction activities, the walk-and-talk process contributes even more to the project.

Lessons learned at Einhorn Yaffee Prescott (EYP) are conducted as breakfast sessions (see Figure 6.1). A professional development committee in each office selects issues or projects that are appropriate for presentation, identifies facilitators, and helps with logistics. Facilitators invite all staff to attend, sometimes drawing almost half of the office.

Rosser International in Atlanta, Georgia, concludes each lessons-learned session by learning more lessons about the process itself. For both evaluative and reinforcement purposes, the firm asks the following questions of people who participate in a session:

> ► Was the time sufficient to discuss the project?

> ► Do you have any advice on how the format should be improved?

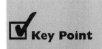

Key Point

Lessons-learned initiatives, reflecting each firm's culture and current priorities, vary in form, frequency, purpose.

EYP/University

Lessons Learned Breakfast Series

Learning Objectives:
- Learn from our mistakes and how to avoid them in the future.
- Understand and be able to implement successful problem-solving strategies.
- Communicate challenges and triumphs in a variety of project phases.

Setting: Informal, interactive gathering, nonconfrontational; no egos please.

When: Last Friday of every month.

Duration: One hour, from 8:30 A.M.– 9:30 A.M.

Material/Format: DO NOT produce any new materials. No need to spend a lot of time preparing for this session. It is informal. Prepare an outline, divide the labor among the project team members so no one has too big of a job. Use existing drawings, sketches, models, and other media created for previous meetings or presentations.

Participants: Principals are off the hook this time. We are looking for key team members who were directly involved, i.e., project managers, project architects, interns, engineers, interior designers. Try to give everyone an opportunity to take part, especially those who wouldn't ordinarily speak.

Suggested Outline:
- **Project History** (10 minutes).
- **Pick Your Challenge** (15–25 minutes) Focus on *one* challenge in any project phase. Describe how the problem occurred; how could it have been avoided; how did the team solve it; *or,* if you haven't solved it yet, brainstorm a solution. The focus could involve one discipline or it could incorporate several disciplines. Try to include as many team members as appropriate.
- **Open Discussion** (20–25 minutes) If the discussion isn't flowing spontaneously, ask for suggestions on how other staff members might have solved the problem or how a similar problem was handled.

Figure 6.1 Lesson-learned guidelines. Courtesy of EYP University.

> ▶ Can you list two changes that could be made in our project processes that would encourage improvement?
>
> ▶ What specifically did you learn about the project discussed today that may help you in future projects?

➤ Would you like to see future projects reviewed for lessons learned?

Handling Fear

Indianapolis, Indiana, firm BSA Architects designed a lessons-learned process expressly to look at project issues on three levels: technical, design, and construction administration. But it faced a challenge common among design firms: how to get people to discuss mistakes? NBBJ's Columbus, Ohio, office dealt with a similar issue by formally recognizing people who offered to share their project issues. At RS&H, the lessons-learned process allays fear by being framed in a positive context. The goal is performance improvement, and PMs focus on smart ideas, effective communications processes, and things that worked. Fingerpointing and negativity are discouraged.

Ayres Associates, of Eau Claire, Wisconsin, discovered that the mere implementation of lessons-learned activities increased the willingness of PMs and team members to share problems. People have become so comfortable with such exchanges that teams sometimes join together to learn lessons. For example, when the firm became concerned that too much reliance was placed on document checking for quality control, lessons learned became a research process. Several teams compared change order activity and requests for information from contractors to see if they could identify opportunities for controlling quality earlier in the project. Teams on renovation and addition projects compared data, as did new construction teams, so that each could establish systems appropriate to their different situations.

Coaching and Lessons Learned

Mavericks and Sole Proprietors

Being a Coach

Practitioners who wish to become leaders must be able to bring people along, whether those people are clients, consultants, or junior staff. But sometimes being an effective coach is tricky, requiring patience when time is short and tolerance for others' style when adherence to standards would expedite work.

Insider Mark Johnson, FAIA: Coaching Colleagues

Mark R. Johnson, FAIA, is Manager, Architectural and Design Marketing for Whirlpool Corporation. Recently, Johnson channeled his personal learning energies into brushing up on coaching skills.

A recent career incarnation consigned me to a new role as mentor and coach for 18 individuals living in 10 states. Equally daunting was the fact that nearly all of them had more experience in the task at hand than did I. The pressure to perform up to expectations was matched only by the adrenaline rush of staying ahead of that many people every day.

Why would a manager be selected for this assignment when his command of the subject matter was nominal? From many companies' perspective, people skills are at a premium, while expertise in a specific subject can be mastered by any number of individuals.

My quick assessment was that the managerial skills of coaching and mentoring were based largely on listening, watching, and focusing on individual motivations. While traveling with my direct reports, I noted their approaches to the same assignment were as different as their DNA. No one solution seemed to be a "best fit" for the whole team. So my approach was to observe individuals' unique way of perceiving and tackling a project, while trying to discern their strengths and weaknesses. Uniqueness is as easy to mistake as weakness. However peculiar they seem to me, their unique traits and rituals were often endearing to clients.

I found breakfast time at Waffle House in the Carolinas to be a great classroom for learning about complementary differences. The vernacular was rich; the regulars were diverse; and everyone enjoyed the company.

Coaching and Lessons Learned

After a client presentation with a protégé, I liked to review the meeting by analyzing our positive accomplishments, then offering constructive criticism on ways to improve the next time. I began with, "What could I have done differently?" Then, "What could we have done differently?" This encouraged my report to self-critique without trepidation. I also found that "carrying a small stick" most of the time made it easier for direct reports to understand the few times when I meant serious business.

My approach to group training was more formal, but included peer coaching, lots of recognition, and a dose of friendly competition. We kept training interactive so team members learned a lot from each other. I often asked subject experts within our team to present. It was an excellent way to identify future leaders, and was exciting to watch them build confidence while sharing an area of expertise. By lauding individual results in front of the group, we reinforced achievement, and everyone instinctively wanted to perform better.

One continuing challenge was discovering and addressing individual motivations, which is key to retaining peak performers and enhancing career enjoyment. It took careful listening and watching, because people grow and motivations change. It was a moving target.

My assignment was not coaching a team of architects in pursuit of projects, but a sales team promoting building products. Since leaving architectural practice to pursue a career in manufacturing, I've been delighted to find the "people" and "process" skills I honed as an architect are highly prized beyond the design profession.

Johnson's approach to coaching reflects the second level of the Involvement Model. As the expert, he structures practice sessions, demonstrates appropriate techniques, observes the novice using the techniques, and provides immediate feedback.

A one-on-one coaching relationship is comfortably established in the course of everyday business and during projects. Often, coaching serves as a preliminary step in a senior staff member's ability to delegate a substantial responsibility to a junior staffer. The expert identifies someone whose skills could be elevated through closely monitored delegation. The two meet to discuss goals, parameters, and time frame. They meet periodically to chart progress, and they

Coaching and Lessons Learned

conduct a final debriefing at the conclusion of the assignment. Written evaluation of the exchange is completed by both participants, so that the facilitator receives feedback on his or her leadership performance, and the novice on his or her skill development. For the coach, an evaluation might include questions such as those listed in Figure 6.2; for the

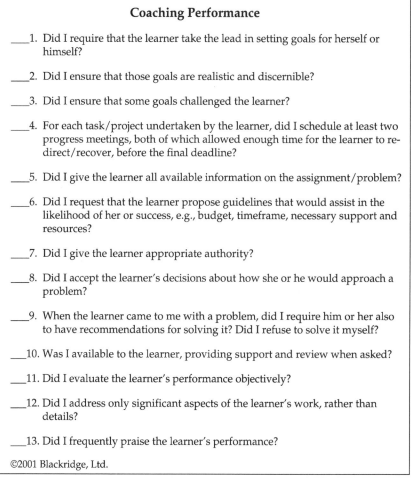

Coaching Performance

___1. Did I require that the learner take the lead in setting goals for herself or himself?

___2. Did I ensure that those goals are realistic and discernible?

___3. Did I ensure that some goals challenged the learner?

___4. For each task/project undertaken by the learner, did I schedule at least two progress meetings, both of which allowed enough time for the learner to redirect/recover, before the final deadline?

___5. Did I give the learner all available information on the assignment/problem?

___6. Did I request that the learner propose guidelines that would assist in the likelihood of her or success, e.g., budget, timeframe, necessary support and resources?

___7. Did I give the learner appropriate authority?

___8. Did I accept the learner's decisions about how she or he would approach a problem?

___9. When the learner came to me with a problem, did I require him or her also to have recommendations for solving it? Did I refuse to solve it myself?

___10. Was I available to the learner, providing support and review when asked?

___11. Did I evaluate the learner's performance objectively?

___12. Did I address only significant aspects of the learner's work, rather than details?

___13. Did I frequently praise the learner's performance?

Figure 6.2 Coaching performance questions.

Learning Performance

___1. Did I achieve the agreed-upon objective?

___2. Was I able to work effectively with others?

___3. Did I seek advice in enough time to use the advice I received?

___4. When I sought advice from my coach, was I always prepared with at least one recommended approach or solution?

___5. Did I allow for unforeseeable delays and mistakes?

___6. Did I ask for all the information I needed?

___7. When I asked for information/support, did I allow enough time for others to respond?

___8. Did I deal with pressure effectively?

___9. Did I periodically report to my coach on the status of my work without having to be asked?

___10. Was I able to listen to negative feedback objectively?

___11. Did I meet all interim deadlines?

___12. Was the quality of my work appropriate?

___13. Do I know what I would do differently next time?

©2001 Blackridge, Ltd.

Figure 6.3 Learning performance evaluation.

learner, an evaluation form might look like the one shown in Figure 6.3.

Finding a Coach

Mavericks also look for ways that they can be coached by others. Even if mavericks practice alone, they engage with some individuals frequently enough to develop learning synergy. In longstanding relationships with business and technical consultants, an architect has a chance to acquire more than facts and data. An architect can ask his or her consultants to walk through steps leading to options, and provide checklists or outlines that the architect can use later to apply information to other situations. For sole proprietors, the most satisfying consultant and vendor relationships evolve when both parties find they are as comfortable coaching each other as they are at being coached. The situation is similar with some clients, builders, craftspeople, and other technical experts, all of whom benefit from synergy with design professionals.

And lessons learned is as productive for sole proprietors as it is for members of design firms. Reflecting on one's own in a deliberate way, and taking the time to record observations and questions, capitalizes on the laboratory nature of projects. Moreover, setting aside a few minutes in project meetings to solicit feedback from clients and colleagues infuses individual practice with new ideas and insights.

Preparing to Learn Some Lessons and Find a Coach

A good way to ensure that you learn valuable lessons and find an appropriate coach is to make a to-do list containing these three tasks:

1. Before you embark on your next project, establish three learning objectives for yourself. Start with the phrase, "By the end of this project I will…" and finish it with a phrase that includes some business or marketing goals, as well as technical learning. For example, "By the end of this project I will…:

   ➤ be aware of at least one new material or system."

> understand my client's business better than I do now."

> be able to use one new feature of my software."

2. At the end of the project, outline your learning in each area and think about learning that occurred spontaneously. To reinforce the latter, the unanticipated learning, ask yourself, "Did I learn anything new about...:

> design or documentation?"

> presentations or marketing?"

> zoning, approvals processes, or the like?"

> other design disciplines?"

> construction?"

> communication or leadership?"

3. As you work through the project, identify one person who might be able to help you improve your knowledge or skill in some area. Arrange a meeting or outside project activity to talk about how he or she could help you incorporate some of his or her expertise into your own practice.

Mentoring

7

Inherent in professionalism is a responsibility of mature practitioners to prepare the next generation to serve in their stead. Also implicit is the reward of leaving a legacy of knowledge. Mentoring is one of the fastest-growing formats for knowledge sharing inside design firms. Long established as a process for helping graduate designers prepare for licensure and for guiding junior staff in their career development, mentor-protégé relationships are increasingly recognized as vigorous knowledge-sharing networks that benefit everyone.

In the Involvement Model shown earlier in Figure 4.5, the mentoring level represents a shift of learning responsibility from the expert to the novice. At the training level, the expert presents a skill or idea to a novice. At the coaching level, the expert works closely with the novice as the new skill is incorporated into practice. At the mentoring level, the novice integrates the expert's knowledge into his or her repertoire and molds it to reflect the novice's personal style. At this point, the expert is a resource for learning, rather than an instructor. In fact, in many firms, the protégé is responsible for initiating the learning engagement with a mentor, rather than the other way around.

A mentor is, however, always mindful of his or her role. Anyone who enjoyed a childhood fascination with Greek mythology recalls the Trojan War and *The Odyssey*. Replete with grotesque monsters, ghosts, natural disasters, steaming battle scenes, and steamy love interests, the epic poem sang of heroes and villains, gore, dying, and eventual victory. The word "mentor" comes from Homer's tale; Mentor was the name of the comrade whom Odysseus charged with the care of his beloved son, Telemachus. Mentor was certainly honored to be entrusted with the guidance and education of the boy; moreover, understanding that Odysseus was a tough warrior prince who did not take things lightly, Mentor would also have felt a certain urgency to do right by Telemachus. Mentoring involves a real commitment to furthering someone's growth and development.

Programs vary widely from carefully constructed relationships, under the guidance of human resources or professional development staff, to loosely defined exchanges that are encouraged, but not monitored. Most mentoring programs are used to help promote the firm's culture, and the firm's culture substantially affects its approach to mentoring.

In any permutation, mentoring serves many purposes in the design professions. It is a:

- Vehicle for career advising and advocacy
- Way of introducing people to broader issues of professional practice
- Means for collectively conducting research and building knowledge within a firm
- Process for stimulating exchange among peers

> Forum for storytelling and sharing the firm's lore

> Source of professional satisfaction for experts and novices alike

This book does not address the Intern Development Program, about which much has been written elsewhere. But whether the goal is to jump-start one's career or to elevate performance through peer efforts, one's own colleagues have a lot to offer.

Finding Good Mentors

Professional growth can be thought of as both vertical and horizontal. In a vertical growth mode, someone strives to learn things to be eligible for promotion, increasing business and communication acumen, as well as technical expertise. In a horizontal mode, the individual focuses on broadening his or her expertise with a goal to achieving complete mastery of a skill or discipline. Whether aspiring to become a generalist or a specialist, a design professional is surrounded by potential mentors (see Figure 7.1).

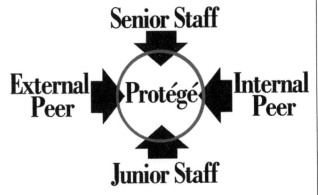

Figure 7.1 Mentors at all levels.

Senior staffers are obvious mentor candidates, but so are peers. Colleagues who were trained differently, who have come from different firms, who work on different projects, and who have different skills can contribute a lot to their peers' knowledge. People outside the firm, whether or not they are involved in projects, offer a world of experience.

Junior employees can be tapped for more than their technological fluency. One design firm raised people's ability to anticipate and manage issues relating to gender and harassment by arranging mentor/protégé roles between some of the firm's senior leadership, all of who were men over 55, with young female designers. The designers were the mentors.

In addition to seeking mentors with various experience levels, one should also look for people with complementary skills. Even inside one's firm, the pool of potential mentors is more like an ocean, as depicted in Figure 7.2.

Within each quadrant, people have much to learn from each other; and between quadrants, the learning potential jumps even higher. What might a hospital designer learn from a marketing professional? What might a PM learn from an administrative assistant? What could a CADD specialist who does a lot of hospital work learn from a construction administrator who does a lot of retail facilities?

Design firm mentor programs seem to encourage protégés to initiate learning relationships, but the ultimate success of the pairing usually rests on the mentor. Area of expertise may be the first criterion for eligibility for mentorship. But character is a close second. To be an effective steward, a mentor must be:

► Objective

► Generous with advice and information

Business Role

Finance
Marketing
Operations
Administration
Human Resources

Expertise

Wet Laboratories
Courthouses
Hospitals
Schools
Retail

Protégé

Discipline

Planning
Architecture
Real Estate Development
Mechanical Engineering
Interior Design
Landscape Architecture

Project Role

Construction Manager
Principal in Charge
Project Manager
Specifications
Designer
CADD

Figure 7.2 Mentor pool.

► Stingy with directions

► Worthy as a role model

► Enthusiastic about honoring and encouraging individual work styles and unique talents

Mentoring exchange is less likely to succeed if a mentor/protégé relationship is forced. Chemistry is critical, and participants need to be able to connect on a personal level. Things are not going well when the mentor does most of the talking or lapses into instruction giving. Similarly, a protégé who seeks out the mentor only in crises, or who seems more interested in just being told what to do, rather than working through options, would be happier in a training mode. Canceled meetings and unavailability are also red alerts for collapsing mentor/protégé pairs.

The true success stories are those relationships in which both parties grow. A couple of examples come to mind:

> A project manager and a principal designer on a store fit-up for a national women's apparel chain provided better service to their client because of a mentor/protégé relationship that they had recently begun. The PM learned about introducing effective design elements into a mundane project by watching the principal, and the principal became more sensitive to working within a client's processes and priorities by talking with the PM.

> A young CADD wizard wanted to learn how to be an effective job captain, and eventually a project manager. He selected a mentor who, it turned out, wanted to understand more about AutoCADD. Each led the other through a training–coaching–mentoring whirlwind, to their mutual delight.

Institutionalizing Mentoring

In the corporate world, mentoring commonly involves experienced professionals providing guidance to ambitious younger staff, like career coaching mentioned in the previous chapter. Many architecture firms encourage such relationships. In addition, because experiential learning is deeply embedded in everyday activity, mentoring has even broader application.

Stewardship programs range from carefully crafted mentoring systems to informal networks, depending largely on a firm's long-range plan and culture. Generally, mentoring frameworks address strategy, matching process, roles and relationships, form/frequency of engagement, and feedback and evaluation.

Strategy

Cannon Design, a 550-person architecture and engineering firm with nine U.S. offices and one in Canada, introduced mentoring in 2000, responding to an employee's suggestion. Today, more than 64 percent of Cannon's employees participate in a carefully designed mentoring program; the firm celebrates an annual mentoring week, and its *Mentoring Today* newsletter is published twice a year. Cannon's recent goals for mentoring were:

> ▶ "To promote the firm's vision and core values.

> ▶ To be a leader in our field and to endure over time by identifying and developing future leaders.

> ▶ To foster an environment of individual learning and help facilitate a learning attitude throughout the organization.

> ▶ To coordinate with other educational initiatives to ensure smooth implementation of professional development."

Leadership development was the focus of HOK's 2001 knowledge-building efforts, and mentoring was a key tactic (see Figure 7.3). The firm had recently refreshed its approach to mentoring, and this sudden emphasis crystallized both the goals and process for expert/novice relationships.

Articulating mentoring strategy helps keep people mindful of the ultimate goal of stewardship, particularly during a pilot program. HOK's statement

☑ **Key Point**

Mentoring frameworks address strategy, matching process, roles and relationships, form/ frequency of engagement, and feedback.

Mentoring   161

Leadership at All Levels

"The organization that will define success and innovation in the 21st Century must have leaders at every level."

— *Peter Druker*

Focus for 2001: Leadership Development
Leadership Convention
Project Manager Basics
Online Skills
Leaders Teaching Leaders
Mentoring

Mentoring Pilot
Mentoring identified by the [AIA Large Firm Round Table] as the Number One strategy for retaining talent.
Identified by [the Executive Committee] as a key HOK strategy.
Retention
Increasing licensed professionals
Improving consistency and quality of work
HOK Pilot Scope ... will include design professionals at the geographic location regardless of market-focus affiliation.
Atlanta
Los Angeles
Dallas
North Central
Florida
Target Audiences
Professionals with 1–5 years of experience
Professionals with 5–10 years of experience
Criteria and expectations
Simple in structure with clearly defined expectations
Training for all participants
Online tracking/documentation/measurement
Critical Success Factors
Defined goals that are meaningful and measurable
100 percent visible management commitment.

Figure 7.3 HOK's 2001 "Leadership at All Levels" program.

presents its rationale for the program, identifies three benchmarks (staff retention, professional licensing, and consistency and quality of work), outlines the pilot, and pinpoints factors that will affect the program's success.

Matching Process

Firms match experts and novices differently. Mentors may pick their protégés or protégés their mentors; or someone else in the firm may play matchmaker. Architecture and engineering firm DLR Group piloted a program that provides considerable latitude to participants, but matches them very carefully. In DLR's 90-person Phoenix office, where mentoring came into its own, the personality and character of the expert and novice drive the process.

Instead of performance appraisals, DLR employees engage in annual career planning sessions with supervisors, during which they agree on professional development goals. As they talk, the supervisor suggests experts who might be helpful in reaching the goals. Subsequently, the supervisor facilitates a match by approaching a potential mentor, considering the likely compatibility with the *mentee* (DLR's preferred terminology), and asking the mentor to initiate a conversation with the mentee, should the latter express discomfort at making the first move.

At Cannon, matching is protégé-driven, although sometimes office leaders urge people with conspicuous star qualities to link up with a specific role model. Working with a mentoring liaison in her/his office, the hopeful protégé completes a mentor request and identifies learning goals and expectations (see Figure 7.4). The liaison then meets with the head of the office to identify an optimum match anywhere in the firm. Cannon encourages cross-office teams on projects, so travel is part of the firm's culture, and videoconferencing a comfortable communications medium.

A few firms have established intense mentoring processes expressly for people with leadership poten-

CANNONDESIGN

Boston ▪ Baltimore ▪ Buffalo ▪ Chicago ▪ Jacksonville ▪ Los Angeles ▪ New York ▪ St. Louis ▪ Vancouver ▪ Washington DC

MENTORING PROGRAM REQUEST FORM

Please complete the following mentoring request form and submit to the mentoring liaison in your office.

Employee name (please print)   Office

What are your specific goals or expectations for the Mentoring Program?

- Meet core competencies for certification, registration or licensure
  - ☐ IDP/Architectural Registration
  - ☐ PE
  - ☐ NCIDQ
  - ☐ Other _____

- Enhance career development
  - ☐ Role modeling
  - ☐ Shared contacts
  - ☐ Career counseling
  - ☐ General support
  - ☐ Other _____

- Build knowledge and skills
  - ☐ Professional
  - ☐ Design
  - ☐ Technical
  - ☐ Client relations
  - ☐ Communication
  - ☐ Leadership
  - ☐ Project management
  - ☐ Presentation
  - ☐ Computer
  - ☐ Other _____

Identify three potential mentors that you would like to request to assist you in meeting these goals:

_____

_____

_____

Please return to the mentoring liaison in your office.

Figure 7.4 Cannon's mentoring program request form. Courtesy of Cannon Design.

tial. Once a year, candidates are mustered, either through personal invitation or by responding to a call for candidates, and invited to select a mentor. Their work may include formal coaching in communications or leadership skills, as well as developing individual leadership styles at the encouragement of their mentor.

Roles and Relationships

To help mentoring thrive, a firm needs to describe generally or specifically what it means by the term *mentor*. At Cannon, a mentor is a role model who is more knowledgeable than the learner, committed to providing guidance and supporting the learner's growth and development, and who identifies developmental opportunities for the protégé. At DLR, the mentor is someone who influences others by passing on knowledge, providing guidance, or helping people attain professional goals.

In addition to defining terms, the firm must also explain who is responsible for moving the process along. The mentor? The protégé? Or is there a process that is so carefully orchestrated that both parties respond to guidelines that keep the relationship on track, like that at HOK, described in the next Insider sidebar. When a protégé is expected to take the lead, an outline or learning plan can be handy, such as that shown in Figure 7.5.

Form and Frequency of Engagement

In either a formal or flexible mentoring program, process matters. The firm should offer guidelines, mandatory or optional, to facilitate the relationship. At HOK, increased structure helped revive a dormant mentoring program.

Mentoring

Personal Protégé Plan

From whom in the firm, or outside it, would you like to learn a new skill, expand your knowledge, or gain a new perspective?

Potential Mentor _____

1. What do you want to learn from this person?
   •

   •

2. What are the opportunities for you to learn from this person?
   •

   •

3. What kind of obstacles stand in either your way or the mentor's?
   •

   •

4. What can you do to reduce the obstacles?
   •

   •

5. Are there any resources or support that will be needed?
   •

   •

6. What steps do you need to take?
   •

   •

   •

7. What is a realistic timeline for this mentoring process?

2000 **B L A C K** R I D G E ,   L T D .   7 8 1 - 2 3 9 - 1 1 1 3

Figure 7.5 Personal protégé plan. Courtesy of Blackridge, Ltd.

Insider Marcia Littell: Mentoring at HOK

Dean of HOKU, Marsha Littell is a specialist in organizational communication and management who was recruited to HOK in 1998 to develop the firm's in-house university. HOKU has emerged as a variegated professional development enterprise and an important contributor to the firm's competitive position. Carefully structured, HOK's new mentoring process represents the kind of deliberate approach that fits the environment of many large firms.

The most requested educational program at HOK is mentoring. Years ago, mentoring was very informal. Senior design or project management or marketing people might "take an interest" in young architects and personally mentor them throughout their career. Our last CEO, Jerry Sincoff, was mentored by founder George Kassabaum. Bill Valentine, HOK president and design chair, was stewarded by Gyo Obata. But as our practice expanded, this process wasn't effective either in growing leaders or in retaining talented young people.

The demand for mentoring increased, and we tried several approaches. All started with fanfare, but within months faded away under the pressure of day-to-day work. Unfortunately, not only were these programs ineffective for the participants, they left behind a cynical attitude about mentoring at HOK.

Several years ago, HOK University facilitated a task force to reinvent mentoring. We looked at previous programs to understand what had worked and what had not. We reviewed the latest thinking outside HOK and considered our particular needs. A HOK program would have to be flexible, so that our varied offices and market-focused groups could tailor it for their needs. It would have to be structured with a clear goal, defined expectations, and frequent "touch points" to keep everyone on track and fix mismatches early. It also couldn't cost too much in time or dollars!

The resulting program calls for a six-month relationship that targets professionals with 0 to 5 and 6 to 10 years of experience as mentees (our people do not like the term *protégé*). Mentors volunteer, then are selected by leadership based on mentee needs. We utilize a personal assessment instrument, the Personal Values Index (PVI), to assess how individuals communicate and learn, and then we match mentors and mentees accordingly.

As their first "touch point," participants attend a half-day training session to understand roles and responsibilities and to execute their personal "mentoring contract." The contract sets out the learning goals and designates meeting frequency, minimally once per month.

At any time, participants can contact their local program coordinator to request a different partner or to discuss a problem. The next scheduled touch point occurs midway into the program, when participants complete online evaluations and attend "what's working/what is not" meetings. Mentees meet together and discuss the program. Mentors meet separately. Themes from these meetings are captured and used to improve the program. At the end of the six-month period, the last touch point involves another online evaluation and brief meeting.

We learn more than we teach through this program. We learned that distance mentoring is not effective at HOK, and that there are never enough "good" mentors to go around. Having learned that the coaching skills of our project professionals needed improvement, we established a process of identifying a coach for each discipline on a project, so that younger people know to whom to look for support.

Our goal is to improve the program and participation every year. Our pilot program was launched in five offices and with almost 75 participants. Evaluations averaged 4.37 on a 5-point scale, and all participants were interested in another six-month stint. Mentoring is growing in our U.S. offices, and HOK London plans to launch the process this year.

Structure helped HOK's program, whereas at DLR, mentoring moved in the opposite direction. Working with a consultant, the firm drafted a program, then beta-tested it. Over time, questions that were originally intended to direct the mentor's work have devolved into discussion points for the mentor/mentee kickoff meeting. Among topics raised for discussion:

➤ What are the opportunities for you to mentor this person in [project management or professional skills]?

➤ What are the mutually acceptable, specific learning objectives?

➤ Which techniques will you employ to mentor him or her to achieve these objectives?

➤ How will you measure success?

➤ How will you provide feedback?

Feedback and Evaluation

Subtle though the effects of mentoring may be, evaluation of the process is important. DLR's program may be informal, but because it is linked to the performance appraisals of staff, mentoring effectiveness is scrutinized every time someone is reviewed. HOK and Cannon provide checkpoints along the way to ensure that experts and novices are comfortable with each other on a personal level, and both firms have formal processes for evaluating the effectiveness of their programs. As Littell mentioned, the last touch point in HOK's process includes completion of essentially identical online evaluation forms by both mentor and protégé (see Figure 7.6).

Both parties to a mentoring relationship should critique their experience, and that information should serve as a lesson learned for each of them, and for the entire program.

Peer Mentoring

Crafted mentoring relationships spur growth for both expert and novice. Among peers, a mutual mentoring attitude, even if it is informal, stimulates learning. Mentoring is about sharing knowledge, facilitating the success of other people, and serving as a resource. And as peers work together on research efforts and new initiatives, their willingness to exchange ideas and information broadens the potential application of mentoring within the firm.

Insider Bonny McLoud, AIA: Peer Mentoring

Bonny McLoud is vice president and a studio leader in Gensler's Houston office. Her experience with Gensler's firmwide committee process reflects the firm's entrepreneurial spirit and regard for group and individual leadership.

To me, peer mentoring means networking and learning from the people with whom you work on leadership initiatives. Gensler has a Knowledge Network comprised of committees that undertake new leadership initiatives. Firmwide there is a Management Committee under which there are four standing sectors: Design and Delivery Systems, Offices, Practice Areas, and Shared Services. Each of these sectors is made up of task forces and steering committees. Task forces are formed to respond to particular goals and operate until their goals have been met, while steering committees have ongoing assignments and guidance responsibilities.

The network is essentially a mentoring enterprise, in which members team to problem-solve, yet learn from each other as they work on a specific initiative. Topics and issues filter up and down through the Management Committee, which is comprised of the Board of Directors, Executive Council, and rotating members. There is an annual calendar of meetings between the Management Committee and specific sectors as deemed important. Specific subjects or issues are assigned to the appropriate leadership sectors for analysis. Committees or task forces establish goals, and members embark upon individual and collective work, proceeding as learners and designing their activities as educational endeavors. Our deliverable is a presentation to the Management Committee of our findings and recommended follow-through.

Committees include senior staff from Gensler offices all over the world. We meet occasionally, and periodic conference calls enable us to guide and support each other and our initiatives. If the Management Committee comes up with an urgent initiative that needs immediate action, they will pass it to the leaders of one of the four other groups, who will address it through conference call meetings. There is a real sense of responsibility within the network, as well as leadership and initiative.

When possible, joint sector meetings are held to stimulate professional exchange among peers, as we prepare and/or deliver our report to the Management Committee. The forum is often a weekend of breakout sessions and presentations to the larger group.

In our own sector, we learn from the people who have particular experience in one market area or delivery system. And we learn from people on other committees or task forces, who may be preparing presentations or publications to help us do our work better. We find out who the experts are and where we can turn within the firm for information. We springboard from our peers' experiences.

Someone said recently that, "Everyone needs two mentors, one 20 years your senior, one 20 years your junior." I would add, "and all the in-between."

HOK Mentoring Program Evaluation
Mentor Form
This is a confidential tool for evaluating this program. Your frank responses are appreciated.
Please fill in the names in your partnership for this program.
Your Name/Office location (Mentor):

_____

Mentee: _____
Note: please fill out an evaluation form for each of your mentees if you have more than one.

Your tenure as a design professional: _____ at HOK: _____

Dates of Mentoring Relationship: _____

1) Is the mentoring program achieving the learning objective you established with your mentee?
- ❏ Yes
- ❏ No
- ❏ Other (Explain)

2) Evaluate each of the following (bold and change the color of your chosen response):

	Poor		Good		Excellent
Quality of meetings with partner	1	2	3	4	5
Quality of program	1	2	3	4	5
How well do you relate with mentee?	1	2	3	4	5
Commitment of mentee	1	2	3	4	5
Value of this experience	1	2	3	4	5

3) What were the two most outstanding elements of this program for you?

4) What most needs improvement in this program?

5) Would you participate again? *(End of Program Evaluation Only)*
- ❏ Yes
- ❏ No

6) Would you like a personal conference with the Program Coordinator to discuss issues?

Figure 7.6 HOK mentor evaluation form.

OWP/P uses peer-group workshops as learning vehicles, studying and promoting best practices related to firm vision, client and project management, and building technology. One such endeavor grew into a substantial learning venture that benefited the original participants and the members of their core market sector group, and influenced thinking throughout the firm.

As part of its vision to enhance design, OWP/P established a task force to define "quality." The task force determined that quality was best defined in comparative terms and that case studies offered the most meaningful way to talk about its attributes. In their search for case studies that reflected quality in the design of K-12 schools, people in the Education Group focused on the integration of facility design with education. Passionate about designing physical environments that facilitate and advance children's creativity and imagination, the group looked to Europe, where school facility design is less economically based than in the United States. After the Vienna school program was identified as a model, eight OWP/P members traveled to Austria to study the schools there and to observe the facilities' impact on the children who attended them. Participants were deliberately selected to represent the firm's diverse members: architects, an engineer, an interior designer, a senior officer, the director of Design, and the head of the Education Group.

The study mission spurred mentoring at two levels. Among the participants, knowledge sharing from the perspective of different disciplines was deep and purposeful, resulting in new programming and planning techniques. Once they returned, they shared their observations with others, both to communicate what they had learned and to reinforce their new knowledge. At this second level, their presentation to the entire office sparked debate and discussion. The posters they created about each school helped them synthesize what they saw and internalize it. "What did we see in Vienna?" has become a theme not just for the participants, but for the entire Education Group. Peer mentoring can be very powerful.

Mavericks and Sole Proprietors

Mavericks and sole proprietors can be great mentors. The perspective of independent practitioners is valuable, differing substantially from the experience of people who practice in traditional settings. And the latitude of a leader of a small firm to generate a mentoring environment is potent.

Insider Jim Wilson, AIA: Mentors and Trust

Several years ago at an AIA program in Galveston, I met a young architect, Jim Wilson, who had just launched his own practice. He carried two business cards, one with the name of his firm and another with the name "X-O studio." He described a vision for an office in which creativity would relate not just to projects, but to people's attitudes. A sole proprietor at the time, and certainly a maverick thinker, Wilson was worth tracking down to find out if such an idea could support a firm and inspire others. It does, and Wilson is a good example of how an entrepreneur can mentor a firm through his vision.

A big, fat *Webster's* dictionary sits on my desk in easy reach at all times. A mentor is "a trusted counselor or guide, a tutor, a coach." Someone who has gray hair, wears spectacles, and speaks calmly and with authority. People listen to mentors.

I never have thought of myself as a mentor, and I sure don't fit my own image of one. Do I counsel, do I guide? Yes, I try to guide others at times; however, more importantly, I realize that every single person in my office is a mentor. Furthermore, I have a new understanding of *Webster's* definition. The word "trust" is key to my new understanding.

When I established my company, Jim Wilson Architects and the X-O studio, I wanted a combination of a traditional architecture firm and a more artistic approach to life. The X-O studio provides mental counterbalance to a traditional architecture office. It is a place where there are no rules, a place to explore, a "laboratory of uncertainty." In the X-O studio, I develop projects simply to stretch my mind, to foster an attitude of curiosity in all of us, to add a little fun to our lives. For our "Tabletop Project" we collaborated with an artist friend to create an object to place on our tabletop. Then, we drew straws to see who went next. Over several weeks, every person in our office created something to add to the project, and it developed into a wonderfully playful exercise. Currently, we are working on a study for a book about the architecture of heaven—a challenging, but fascinating, endeavor.

The mission of our firm is "to be a positive force in the world *through* architecture." "Through" is italicized to stress the practice of architecture as only a vehicle through which we can achieve our primary mission: to be a positive force in the world. I believe that architecture is, most important, about life. I try to encourage my teammates to pursue a full life. Just as I do, they have families, social lives, dreams. I want architecture to be a part of their lifestyle, not just a job. I want them to find fulfillment in the work that they do. I want them to develop their minds, develop friendships, create good memories.

People work with me, not for me. I don't consider myself "the boss" or "the leader"; I see myself walking side by side with a group of professional individuals, sharing what we know, adding our expertise to the mix. We are a team of mentors. There is a young guy in our office who knows more about construction and codes than anyone else I have ever worked with. He is invaluable to our team, and freely shares his knowledge. There is our computer guru. He knows stuff about computers that most of us don't even want to know, and we are all glad he is here. We have an office manager who knows our contracts inside and out, and she frequently quizzes us about our services, keeping us on our toes, guiding us. We have a summer intern whose quiet enthusiasm, creativeness, and subtle actions challenge us in magically special ways.

I pass on responsibility—a lot of it. I can do this is because of the mutual trust engendered in our office. It isn't easy to release responsibility to others. Mistakes will be made. But I truly believe that each one makes us stronger, better. At our office, "Use your best judgment" is our only rule.

I am surrounded by mentors. They don't have gray hair, and some of them are very, very quiet. I have found that mentors work best by setting an example. They are the people who work with me, side by side, every day. As my mentors, they are the people I trust.

Two of the great benefits of mentoring are the trust and camaraderie the relationship stimulates among participants.

Mentoring is a convenient way for individuals to contribute to their profession. Through one-on-one relationships, committee work, community involvement, and the like, an individual can foster someone else's professional growth and enjoy peer mentoring opportunities at the same time.

Implementation

8

The top priority of an internal professional development program is to hone the firm's competitive edge. To this end, as discussed in the previous chapters, the firm begins with a clear educational strategy, based on its unique long-range business plan for professional practice.

With the strategy in mind, the firm assesses the kind of knowledge that will provide the greatest value for its clients, its staff, and its own institutional well-being. Then it designs a proprietary program

Figure 8.1 The implementation element. © 2002 Blackridge, Ltd.

for building and sharing such knowledge. As designed, the program will stimulate professional exchange between novices and experts throughout the firm, draw fresh ideas and perspectives from the world outside the firm, and inspire individual growth among all its members. Now the trick is to implement this program.

Insider George C. Grigg, AIA: Starting an In-House University

George Grigg, AIA, is a board member and principal with Gresham, Smith and Partners. Grigg initiated planning of an internal continuing educational program, as a result of the firm's 1996 strategic plan. By 2000, the firm had a Committee for Learning and an identity, EXCEL, an acronym for: EXcellence through Continuous Education and Learning. By 2002, the firm had won the AIA/Continuing Education System large firm Award for Excellence.

I believe that the key to beginning a successful educational program in a design practice is to treat the creation of the program as a project. This should not be confused with the administration of the educational program, but the process by which a program is developed, bought into by the firm, and put into place.

I used our project management process as my model for initiating the continuing education (CE) program at Gresham, Smith and Partners. Project Planning at GS&P is a five-step process. The first step is the scope of work. In our CE situation, the scope of work included an initial assessment and needs analysis to determine what management wanted to accomplish through an in-house educational program. Once this scope was agreed upon, the other four steps fell into place.

I served as "project manager (PM)" and "principal in charge (PIC)," just as in many GS&P design projects. As project manager, I developed the task list (work breakdown structure.) This breakdown was the basis of the schedule. Responsibilities were assigned, and the investment was calculated to accomplish this initial "scope of work." I presented the project budget and schedule to the firm's management, and the work began.

In typical project format, at the completion of the first phase, the client—in this case, the firm management—was presented with the results of the effort and a recommendation regarding the next steps. As PM and PIC, I recommended a program with six initiatives. During review with the firm management, we decided to implement four of the initiatives in the coming year. At this point, we took a senior project manager off line and assigned our professional development project to her under my direction as the principal in charge.

The "project" was more clearly defined, the next phases were authorized by the "client," and we had a dedicated "PM" in place, so it was time to move to the next phase. Again, the project was planned with a scope of work, work breakdown structure, schedule, roles and responsibilities, and budget. "Design" commenced.

The project came on line with GS&P's first classes offered in the first quarter, and the fourth educational initiative having its first class early the following year. At that point, the project/program was up and running. The firm then transitioned the project manager back onto projects and we acquired a program director/training manager, like a client's facilities director, to manage the program. Our training manager continues to work to improve the program, as it becomes more a part of the firm's culture under my ongoing role as principal in charge. I am also the "client representative," as the firm uses the programs that are developed.

Implementation Timeline

As George Grigg points out in the Insider sidebar, the initial implementation of a proprietary learning program is a project similar to any significant, multi-layered commission a firm might undertake. Large firms are convinced that it is most difficult for them to roll out a quality professional development program, because of the sheer complexity of their endeavor. Small firms observe that, even though their "significant" project is modest by comparison, their lack of resources for retaining consultants or capturing staff time makes their hurdles higher than anyone else's. And midsized firms know that, as in all other things, they face greater challenges than their counterparts at either end of the size spectrum.

When it comes to implementing a proprietary learning program, however, they are all in the same boat. No matter how simple or complex the practice, design firms seem to need at least two years to imple-

Key Point

No matter how simple or complex the practice, design firms seem to need at least two years to implement a professional development program that reflects their goals.

ment a professional development program that reflects their goals. The Implementation Timeline laid out in Figure 8.2 pertains to firms of any size, both in terms of the essential tasks and minimal time needed to complete them. The following subsections delve into each increment in turn.

Education Committee (EDCOM) Charge

For purposes of both tapping appropriate perspectives and building support, an education committee (EDCOM) is effective in leading and promoting professional development in design firms. As discussed in Chapter 2, EDCOM creates the professional development plan, monitors its implementation, and oversees quality. Supporting EDCOM are individuals or task forces to help with specific activities; and, for firms with multiple locations, local committees for ongoing support and insight. One of the first things EDCOM will take up is its own nomenclature: Education Committee or something else?

In most firms, the education chair, or director, is at the principal or associate level, and the committee includes department representatives and people who can speak knowledgeably about firm leadership, marketing, intern development, professional development and adult education, human resources, quality assurance, reference and sample libraries, and information technology.

EDCOM establishes a meeting schedule, and members must be prepared to commit time to the effort. Rotating membership on an annual or biennial basis provides a stream of fresh ideas, as well as an end in sight for people who are working hard on the committee. Some firms set attendance requirements for EDCOM meetings, determining that people who

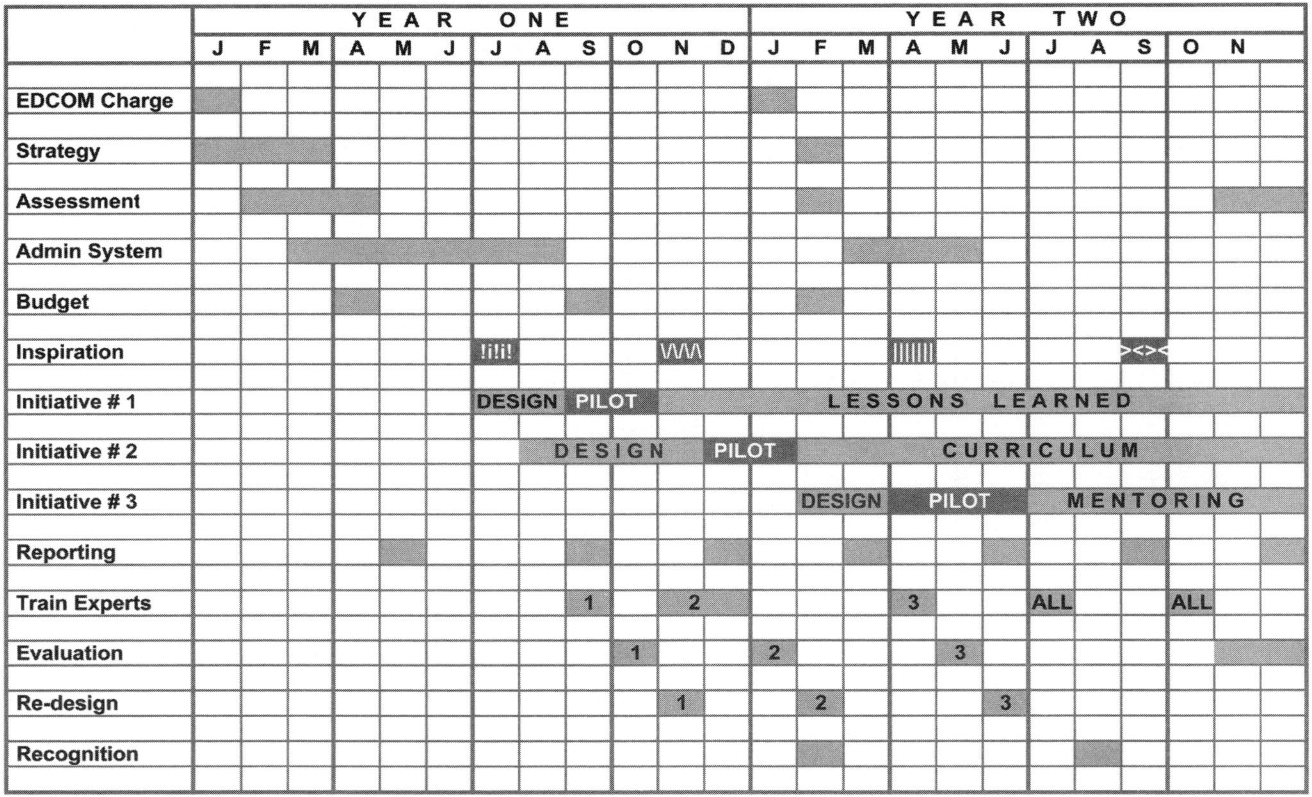

Figure 8.2 Implementation Timeline. © Blackridge, Ltd.

cannot participate consistently should be replaced by others who can. Such a policy is probably wise, particularly in the early development stages of a program.

EDCOM's progress is greatly facilitated if one of its first actions is to register the firm as a provider with the AIA's Continuing Education System. AIA/CES is on the cutting edge of state requirements for continuing education. The processes it has in place can serve as models for the firm's own systems. The *CES Provider Manual* is an excellent resource for information and ideas on program development and management, and it is updated yearly. And AIA/CES staff are both knowledgeable and accessible to firms.

The Implementation Timeline allows a month for development of EDCOM's charge. If a charge is presented to EDCOM by the firm's leadership, then the committee will need some time to refine and clarify the charge. If leadership doesn't charge EDCOM, then EDCOM develops its own purpose. Although most firms expect EDCOM to be responsible for program execution, some organizations rely on EDCOM only for strategy, assessment, record-keeping, overall evaluation, and general educational frameworks. Each department or office then develops its own professional development activities within the structure. In any case, communication of the educational goals, EDCOM composition, and charge is the first of many reports the committee issues, some just to the firm's leadership, others firmwide.

EDCOM's charge is reviewed and revised each year, to reflect the firm's evolution.

Strategy

Sketching out an initial strategic plan for knowledge building, as discussed in Chapter 2, can probably be

Key Point

For design firms, appointment of an Education Committee to create the professional development plan, monitor its implementation, and oversee quality not only taps appropriate perspectives, but also builds support for professional development. The timeline allows a month annually for charging the committee.

accomplished within three months, while EDCOM defines its charge and begins assessment of learning needs and opportunities.

Strategy includes a compelling motivation for professional development. Strategy might tie learning to the firm's business goals and to people's issues and concerns, or it might position learning as a refresher and a spark for new ideas. Or the strategy could be to connect learning to career advancement within the firm. EDCOM summarizes how professional development will relate to the firm's human resources practices, especially performance appraisals; to the firm's quality assurance processes; to its design and project delivery system; and to its client service approach.

One important strategic question is mandatory involvement:. Is participation in the firm's professional development program a requirement for continued employment? For promotion to a managerial position? For eligibility for associate or principal status? Is completion of certain activities required for some positions? Do all employees, principals included, have learning mandates, as is the case at FreemanWhite, NBBJ, and Gresham Smith? Or does the firm prefer a goal, like HOK's minimum of 40 hours per year per employee, which might later covert to a requirement? The decision will reflect the firm's culture and values.

Another important question is event scheduling. The demands of people's personal lives affect their ability to participate in activities outside the normal workday. Most firms rely on the 11:30 A.M. to 1:30 P.M. time frame for structured classes and seminars. Establishing such general parameters during the strategy phase makes it easier for EDCOM to proceed and for future learners to use the system.

> ☑ **Key Point**
>
> As EDCOM establishes strategy it must:
>
> ▶ Identify staff's compelling motive for knowledge building,
>
> ▶ Link learning to professional activities.
>
> ▶ Determine the degree to which participation in learning events is mandatory.
>
> ▶ Decide standard time frames for scheduling activities during the week.
>
> ▶ Set an appropriate balance between internally generated events and externally generated ones.
>
> ▶ Plan for marketing professional development to staff.

This is also the time for EDCOM to take a position on the degree to which internally generated learning programs will dominate people's professional development. The point of a proprietary program is to help differentiate the firm in the marketplace, therefore probably at least half of each employee's professional development time should be generated by the firm. But part of a healthy learning dynamic is the introduction of outside perspectives. Many firms set aside monies for people's use in attending conferences or pursuing individual initiatives outside the firm, and most firms invite manufacturers and outside experts to provide educational seminars at the firm's offices. Years one and two may involve a disproportionately large share of vendor workshops as the firm develops and tests its own.

During strategy efforts, EDCOM must also address its approach to marketing professional development to all employees. New staff orientation may be an opportunity to explain the firm's program to employees as they enter the firm. Email bulletins, printed or electronically transmitted newsletters, and brochures appeal to design professionals. Public recognition and positive feedback are very effective ways to generate enthusiasm for the program.

The Implementation Timeline includes a shorter period for strategy in year two. Then, and thereafter, revisions to educational strategy can probably be accomplished within one month following EDCOM's charge.

Assessment

In years one and two, assessment of learning needs and opportunities merits considerable attention through three assessment periods. The first one allows intense investigation near the beginning of the first year when multiple levels of the Assessment Pyramid (Figure 3.2) should be researched, as described in Chapter 3. The information accumulated from the assessment is presented to the firm's leadership as part of EDCOM's first progress report.

The second assessment period allows a concise investigation of one additional level of the pyramid near the beginning of year two. At the end of year two, and every year thereafter, thoughtful comparison and review of assessment data occur, so that information will be available when EDCOM is charged when the next year begins.

Administrative System

Implementation relies on user-friendly administrative infrastructure, and for most firms that means intranet processes, which employees can use to view educational offerings online, identify dates and times, register to participate, select lunch, or enroll on a different date or in an entirely different program, if the first choice is full. The program immediately appears on the staff members' calendars, and an electronic reminder alerts them on the day of the event. After the session, they evaluate it online, and their successful completion is confirmed by receipt of an emailed certificate or by review of their updated transcripts. Such a system is friendly to learning experts, too, as they deliver and facilitate events. Experts submit proposals online, review registration, receive attendance lists prior to the session and evaluations shortly thereafter, and document their programs for electronic archiving.

Regardless of the medium, reporting processes are crucial to the firm's professional development

Key Point

In assessing the firm's learning needs and opportunities, EDCOM should research at least four of the levels of the Assessment Pyramid (refer back to Figure 3.2) within the first two years: the firm's long-range plan, clients and markets, external signals, performance, and/or staff review.

Tip

Software for administering in-house professional programs for design firms has been developed by a number of organizations. At least one, by Professional Development Network, Inc., may be available for sale. Investigate the possibilities before you invest in system development.

program, because reports are required for external use, employee use, and the firm's use. Simplicity and clarity are key.

The most critical reporting system is the one for external reviewing bodies, such as licensing and certification boards; professional societies like AIA, ASID, ASLA; quality assurance groups like the International Organization for Standardization; and finance and insurance companies, and the like. If staff members count on the firm's program to help them meet professional requirements, then the firm must develop processes for reporting continuing education information in terms and formats acceptable to reviewing bodies. A summary list of all applicable reviewing bodies, their annual continuing education requirements, their annual reporting deadlines, and identification of any required report format must be updated at least annually, as organizations and licensing agencies frequently amend requirements.

Reviewing bodies occasionally request supplemental information about educational programs and employee activity. For that reason, and for the firm's own use, a complete history of the professional development program is maintained. Every firm-generated event is documented in terms of dates, times, location, provider or internal facilitator, content outline and learning objectives, number of professional development hours, HSW status, attendee list, as well as samples of tests, visuals, handouts, evaluation results, and certificates of completion. If the AIA/CES or a state architectural registration board decides to audit the firm's program, information must be up to date and easy to understand.

Another reporting system is employee-focused, summarizing individuals' continuing education

Key Point

The most critical reporting system is that which tracks, records, and reports data of interest to licensing and certification boards, professional societies, and other external reviewing bodies.

progress in a format similar to a college transcript. Staff use this information to confirm their records, prepare for internal performance appraisals, report to those agencies not already contacted by the firm, and for other education-related matters.

The third reporting system is for the firm's use in tracking, reporting, and archiving the entire program. Information like that collected in Freeman White's sample of courses, shown in Figure 5.1, can encapsulate data about courses and seminars, lessons-learned programs, special research initiatives and study tours, and the like. Individual learning activities performed within the context of the firm, such as research involved in designing a course, would appear on transcripts, and the output would typically be archived by the individual. Activities performed under the auspices of a different AIA/ CES provider, such as vendors or AIA and SMPS

ABCAdvance Employee Transcript

Name: Samuel Diescher
Employee Number: 111

Professional Registrations/Certifications	Registration Numbers
Ohio	33033

Professional Memberships	Member Numbers
American Institute of Architects	000300000
Society for Marketing Professional Services	3003

Course Number	Name	Completion Date	Location	Provider	Hours	HSW?
PM011	Project Financial Management	3/11/03	ABC	Vincente	4	Y
LL021	Lessons Learned: Mercy Hospital	2/21/03	Mercy Hosp.	Nu & Brooks	2.5	Y
M103	Trends in Higher Education	2/13/03	ABC	Roop	2	N
S231	Elements of Green Roofing	1/16/03	ABC	Building Logics, Inc.	1.5	Y

Figure 8.3 Sample transcript.

chapters, must be clearly distinguished, so that professional staff do not have to duplicate reporting to agencies and other reviewing bodies.

In addition to reporting processes, scheduling systems are important, not just for allocating time slots and physical facilities, but also for ensuring that registered professionals are able to meet state requirements within designated time frames. Currently, fewer than half the states that mandate continuing education use the calendar year for reporting purposes. For many, June is the filing cutoff. A few states close out in February or July. Some states have rolling deadlines, so that professionals must file continuing education data by the anniversary of their registration. To address such inconsistency, firms are wise to distribute learning opportunities throughout the year.

For AIA/CES-registered providers and some other external reviewing bodies, scheduling also triggers formal notification about events. Prior to an event, the firm submits an application or description to the reviewing organization, so that participants may receive appropriate credit upon completion. The firm must honor the form and deadlines requested by external organizations.

The Implementation Timeline assumes that half of year one will be devoted to creating and implementing an administrative infrastructure to support the firm's knowledge-building enterprise. In year two, after revisions to the educational strategy and assessment of new learning needs, the firm may need only three months to revise and further develop its support systems. In years three and four, infrastructure is likely to continue to need substantial attention as the firm's program evolves. But once the firm has established a program that is both consistent and flexible enough to satisfy its learning goals, adjustments to administrative processes will demand much less attention.

Budgeting

All firms desire a program that balances economy and effectiveness, whether the professional development budget is 4 percent of total firm revenues, like that of FreemanWhite Academy, or a modest fixed dollar amount for hard costs, plus whatever time the champions for professional development can dedicate.

If the firm has a short track record in professional development, the work of creating a budget proceeds almost continually throughout the first year, as EDCOM develops educational strategies, assesses learning needs and opportunities, and sets priorities. From the start, EDCOM takes the initiative in estimating, recording, and reporting costs, explaining the contribution of each investment to the firm's educational goals. Most anxieties about spiraling overhead costs can be allayed by volunteered status reports.

Time is, of course, the largest cost. To set the right tone, and to inform future budgets, EDCOM tracks its own time. In addition, all principals, associates, technical and administrative staff who are involved in developing and operating the firm's proprietary program record their time, probably working in some or all of the following areas:

▶ Strategy and assessment
▶ Organization and administration
▶ Planning and design of major initiatives, including training the experts

> Design, delivery, and evaluation of individual events

> Evaluation and improvement of the overall program

> Marketing the program and events

Hard costs vary widely, and firms may show line items like any of the following in their professional development budgets:

> Salaries of staff dedicated full or part time to continuing education

> Their travel

> Their training

> Office supplies

> Telephone

> Subscriptions, reference materials

> Consulting fees

> Speaker fees

> Photography

> Copies and reproduction

> Presentation materials

> Facilities and equipment

> Food and beverage

> Information and communications technology

> Software

Distinct from the costs associated with developing and managing the professional development program are those that reflect employee participation in it. In terms of time, staff engagement in the firm's proprietary curriculum, lessons-learned sessions, mentoring programs, and similar activities must be tracked as carefully as their traditional continuing education activities, such as conference attendance

☑ **Key Point**

The critical "budgeting" issue is whether or not the firm actively encourages participation in its professional development program. Employees become first confused, and then cynical, when a stated goal for knowledge building is continually undermined by a demand for 95 to 100 percent billability.

and outside training. In terms of hard costs, professional development budget items may include association dues and attendance costs, professional registrations, conference and convention attendance, tuition reimbursement, site visits and study tours. Allowances for some individual learning initiatives and special events may also be set aside.

Firms differ in how they compensate staff for time spent in continuing education. It is quite common for staff to use their lunchtime to take advantage of the firm's program, matching their contribution of time with the firm's contribution of the program. In any case, compensation policies need to be clear, and typically they are.

Fog is more likely to settle over the relationship between project staffing and the firm's continuing education priorities. Employees become first confused, and then cynical, when a stated goal for knowledge building is continually undermined by a demand for 95 to 100 percent billability. Staff deployment charts must include appropriate allocation of professional development time to meet the firm's stated objectives. Department and project managers' performance appraisals need to assess their effectiveness in supporting staff's achievement of the firm's learning goals.

Part of EDCOM's budgeting process should also involve tracking return on investment. Return might be expressed in many ways—as the number of professional development hours achieved by employees, number of new professional registrations, increase in retention, decrease in change orders, or any benchmark meaningful to the firm. Some firms position professional development as a modest revenue generator by opening programs to other firms or clients

 Bright Idea

Tom Peters reminds people in professional service firms that:

➤ "We are in the knowledge business. Period.

➤ Sharing is not automatic. Period.

➤ We need a simple structure and clear incentives to foster sharing. Period.

➤ We need human beings to help extract and package the 'knowledge.' Period."
[Peters, 1999]

for a fee, selling workbooks or course outlines, consulting to other organizations, or the like. Whether or not the firm is so ambitious, presentation of program costs should always be balanced by a presentation of its accomplishments.

The Implementation Timeline proposes that a preliminary budget be set by the beginning of the second quarter of year one, based on EDCOM's strategy and information formed during the assessment. Five months later, with an administrative system in place and design of two learning programs well under way, the budget can be adjusted for the remainder of the year. Again five months later, now into year two, a budget for the entire year can be proposed.

Inspiration

Design firms are creative places. A program for knowledge building should inspire new ideas and accommodate pursuit of them; for example, a field trip to Vienna, like OWP/P's initiative; a design competition; research about facilities for Alzheimer's patients; a symposium on rebuilding a war-torn country. Topics like these arise spontaneously, and many should be pursued. The Implementation Timeline anticipates such unprogrammable opportunities, and a realistic budget should allow for them.

Professional Development Initiatives

The Implementation Timeline suggests how three major learning initiatives might be introduced over two years. The design phase involves not only EDCOM, but also task forces comprised of managers and experts who are likely to be invited to serve as trainers, coaches, and mentors. Since the firm's entire professional development program relies on

Key Point

Design firms are creative places. A program for knowledge building should inspire new ideas and accommodate pursuit of them.

the effective participation of senior staff, it must be designed to invite and support them.

For each initiative, design is followed immediately with the launch of a carefully monitored pilot. Test cases for lessons learned might involve one or two projects. For curriculum, one internally developed course and a few workshops conducted by AIA/CES vendor providers might supply sufficient feedback prior to wider rollout. The mentoring pilot might start with one or two pairs. Although the effectiveness of the mentoring approach probably won't be measurable within just three months, participants will be able to comment on the usefulness of processes and guidelines.

In the pilot phase, learners, as well as facilitators, have an opportunity to critique the learning event from their perspective. Pilots also shed light on the accuracy of budgets and the efficacy of administrative systems. It's usually about halfway through a pilot that the need for additional protocols and checklists becomes apparent. Things can slip through the cracks at a small firm as well as at a large one. Lukmire Associates' seminar planning checklist, shown in Figure 8.4, was one of the tools praised by the AIA/CES jury that honored the firm in 2000.

A pilot helped one firm recognize that course designers need deadlines for their submittal of seminar proposals, content outlines, visuals, and handouts in advance of their session. A pilot is also the best time to discover that back-up instructors should be lined up for every event, because a room full of increasingly impatient staff is expensive in terms of wasted time and eroding interest. Perhaps most important, pilots ignite interest in, and enthusiasm for, the firm's in-house professional development program.

Key Point

In the pilot phase, learners, as well as facilitators, have an opportunity to critique the learning event from their perspective.

Lukmire Partnership Seminar Planning Checklist

☐ Select presenter for program.

☐ Coordinate and schedule date with presenter.

☐ Determine program content, learning objectives, and teaching method with presenter.

☐ Determine with presenter the "props" required for presentations, learning aids, A/V materials, material samples, etc.

☐ Black out date to reserve main conference room.

☐ Develop poster for advertisement of seminar.

☐ Determine appropriate participants other than office architectural staff.

☐ Hang poster on office events bulleting board and send via email.

☐ Determine Learning Unit Hours and determine if requirements are met for HSW.

☐ Register programs (AIA/CES "Form A").

☐ Provide on-site signup reporting forms (AIA/CES "Form B").

☐ Send menu for lunch to participants.

☐ Set up conference room with the props required for presentation, learning aids, A/V materials, material samples, etc., as determined by each presenter.

☐ Order lunch and have delivered.

☐ Set up conference room for seminar (table and chair setup, A/V, etc.).

☐ Send in AIA/CES Form B to University of Oklahoma.

☐ Produce In-house Seminar Series Learning Unit/Hours Transcript.

☐ Produce and distribute Certificate of Completion to seminar participants.

©Lukmire Partnership

Figure 8.4 Lukmire Partnership seminar planning checklist. © Lukmire Partnership

Reporting

EDCOM regularly prepares and presents reports about the firm's lifelong learning enterprise. The timeline suggests one when the assessment and initial budget have been completed, another four months later, after initial administrative systems have been installed and while the first major initiative is being beta-tested. Reports include accomplishments, prob-

     Implementation

lems and their solutions, recommended changes, revised budgets and schedules, concerns, and cries for help. Unless the firm employs staff dedicated exclusively to developing the educational program—and even if it does—EDCOM should actively seek to identify tasks and spread them around the firm. People are more likely to appreciate and support a venture in which they have a hand, and they are more likely to able to help if they have small, discrete functions to perform.

In the timeline, the first report is followed by quarterly updates, which are not necessarily issued to the same people. Some reports may be reserved for EDCOM, some for firm leadership, others distributed to everyone. The format—memos, email bulletins, graphic presentations, newsletters—is less important than meaningful information. But in the first few years of the program, EDCOM and firm leadership monitor the program closely and report their observations.

Key Point

The first program report should probably be made as soon as the assessment and initial budget have been completed.

Train the Experts

During implementation, EDCOM forms a process for identifying, training, and reviewing the performance of the experts who develop and facilitate learning events. At first, the temptation is simply to solicit volunteers. As a result, EDCOM may be faced with the greater challenge of stimulating technical gurus to care at least as much about the people they propose to educate as they do for their subject matter. Professional development is ultimately about inspiring people to do things differently. It is not simply about giving them information. Skills in communication, presentation, and the engagement of learners must be taught to people who lack them.

Even senior staff prefer the annoyance of mandatory rehearsals or beta-tests to the humiliation of poor evaluations.

The timeline indicates that facilitators for the first and second initiatives, lessons learned and mentoring, will be coached as they begin their pilot sessions, but this assumes that they have been involved in the design of the programs, too. If they have not, their training occurs before the pilot. In any case, EDCOM members make good guinea pigs for these sensitive initiatives. Curriculum experts begin training before the pilot, and their coaching support continues well into the pilot launch.

Once the first group of experts has been prepared for the various pilots, then training occurs on a more regular basis, perhaps quarterly, for all new facilitators. In the future, as the program is well established, train-the-experts may be slated as a quarterly or semiannual undertaking.

Evaluation

Evaluation during the first two years focuses on participant feedback about each major initiative once during the pilots and again when the entire program is reviewed during the end of the second year.

EDCOM reviews critiques about individual events, including the train-the-experts effort, as they are completed. By the last quarter of year two, the committee should be able to report on such benchmarks as the number of staff participating in the program, number of learning units completed, cost per participant, trends in program evaluations, and the like. In subsequent years, a full year-end evaluation will include progress on strategic goals, like those discussed in Chapter 2, as well as on specific initiatives. The information will then be available to EDCOM when it is charged and involved in strategy setting for the new year. *Note*: Evaluation is discussed in detail in Chapter 9.

Redesign

The primary purpose of professional development programs is improvement. No matter how much hard work has gone into launching the firm's continuing education program, only additional hard work will keep it alive. The Implementation Timeline conspicuously identifies redesign in years one and two, following evaluation of each major initiative. In subsequent years, redesign of the overall program and administrative systems occurs in the first or second quarter, after EDCOM has set strategy, and with fresh information provided through the recently completed evaluation.

Recognition

The final category on the timeline, recognition, is a form of marketing that uses rewards and incentives to stimulate people's enthusiasm in, and commitment to, the program. Meaningful programs assist people to perform their jobs well and take on increasing responsibility. In firms that take quality improvement seriously, people's continuing professional development earns them greater authority, increased compensation, and eligibility for promotion over the long term, all of which are powerful incentives and rewards.

In the short term, however, recognition still fuels the professional development engine. Certificates of completion, which might be created through an in-house design competition, offer immediate acknowl-

Key Point

After the program has been in place for a few years, evaluations will include participant feedback, benchmark data, and progress on strategic educational goals.

Key Point

No matter how much hard work has gone into launching the firm's continuing education program, only additional hard work will keep it alive.

Key Point

In firms that take quality improvement seriously, people's continuing professional development earns them greater authority, increased compensation, and eligibility for promotion over the long term, all of which are powerful incentives and rewards.

edgment of individual investment in professional growth. Office meetings can feature the accomplishments of individuals and the overall program. Principals can conspicuously bestow office T-shirts and mugs on staff members who actively participate in the firm's program.

And, most important, every employee's annual review should include continuing education as a performance criterion, either for the job he or she currently holds or the one to which he or she aspires. Requesting staff members to state their goals for professional growth, and meaningfully recognizing individuals' success in reaching those goals, are the most potent stimulants for professional development that the firm can administer.

The timeline proposes two formal recognition events in year two of program rollout, after several evaluations have been performed and two initiatives are firmly in place. In following years, formal recognition should occur at least twice a year, if not quarterly.

Mavericks and Sole Proprietors

For mavericks and sole proprietors, implementation is actually the easiest element of the professional development cycle—provided you don't bite off more than you can chew, of course.

Insider Andy Pressman, FAIA: The Cyclone Approach

The implementation process for mavericks and sole proprietors reflects the individual's specific professional goals and unique personality. When architects' passions are unleashed, they can, and do accomplish a great deal. Andy Pressman, FAIA, has chosen multiple career paths within the profession of architecture. He has his own practice; he teaches and is director of the Architecture Program at the University of New Mexico; and

---

he has written five books, including Architectural Design Portable Handbook *(McGraw-Hill, 2001) and* The Fountainheadache *(John Wiley & Sons, Inc., 1995). In the profile here, Pressman interviews himself to share his learning process and to . . . see what it would be like to be featured in one of those advertisement "personality profiles."*

What phrase do you repeat too often?

"Everything's a design problem."

Favorite movie?

Joe versus the Volcano. That tropical island is my fantasy: Jewish natives who love Orange Crush and get massaged with dead fish slapped on their backs, drinking coconut milk and eating mangos.

Okay, back to reality. I'd love your perspective on professional development in the realms of teaching, writing, and practice. How do you do this? Better yet, why do you do this?

First and foremost, I'm an architect, and passionate about doing design. I discovered that teaching was incredibly stimulating, and that the academic environment provided a venue for the discussion of ideas. It was difficult for me to find time to reflect and think while exclusively in an office context. Writing presents an extraordinary challenge, with the possibility of failing miserably and making a great fool of myself. But, as the cliché goes, without risk, without failure, there is no growth, professional or otherwise. Writing has become another mode of creative expression, similar to other artistic endeavors, that helps me to discover and communicate meaning in design.

So, basically, you're implementing the "cyclone approach to lifelong learning."

Yes. All these activities are synergistic, inform each other, and infuse my work with excitement, energy, and passion for engaging new architectural challenges or for examining mundane architectural projects in new ways.

Let's get personal. Jean's readers want to know: What's your best suit?

Ermenegildo Zegna. It's mostly the material, but I like the cut.

Briefly describe yourself.

Reluctant sex symbol and sensitive male of the new millennium.

Which computer do you use?

Titanium Mac PowerBook G4.

Which car do you drive?

Titanium Honda Civic hatchback, 1996.

What else contributes to your professional development?

I think that design competitions are one of the most enlightening continuing education strategies, because they offer the freedom and luxury to push the design envelope. At best, a new commission and/or publicity can be secured; at worst, losing schemes can enhance a marketing portfolio. I'm batting .500. I won an open competition, lost an invited competition. My losing scheme is featured in my latest book and I pity the fool who did not select it. I also discuss some of my design strategies with students and colleagues and see how it could have maybe evolved. You spend more time on something, it usually gets better.

Favorite ice cream?

Cookies 'n Cream. Here's a professional development/urban design lesson derived from dessert:. The higher the Oreo-to-ice-cream ratio (O:IC), the better. Dense clusters of intense-flavored cookie, followed by minimalist vanilla, dramatize the contrast, yielding the most satisfaction. Also, the skillful use of these different materials coalesces in an artful composition that touches all the senses, and the soul.

What motivated you to teach and write?

I'd like to say it was intellectual curiosity, as well as the noble idea to give something back and help students. The real reason was I needed extra cash to augment income from my fledgling young firm. But, amazingly, in spite of myself, I've been extremely fortunate to structure a situation that is sometimes quite satisfying, always difficult, and provocative.

The cyclone approach is adopted by many mavericks, because learning opportunities are everywhere and often coincide with marketing opportunities. The jaws of public committees and boards yawn for design professionals. Slots open up on award juries and convention panels. And in corners, books and magazines pile up, waiting to be explored.

The Implementation Timeline still pertains, however, for individuals who want to balance long-term goals, such as writing a book, with immediate learning opportunities. When in doubt, map it out. Then select one or two long-term professional development initiatives for dedicated pursuit, as you reserve time along the way for unanticipated chances to grow. As Pressman suggests, satisfying plus difficult plus provocative is not a bad learning environment for a design professional.

Evaluation

9

The fifth element, evaluation, addresses the success of two factors: the various pieces of the learning system itself, and the learning that actually is accomplished by participants.

Evaluating the Learning System

Among the pieces of the system that should be evaluated are those reflected in Implementation Timeline, introduced in Chapter 8.

> ▸ How well has EDCOM done its job?

> ▸ Are the assessment processes generating useful information?

> ▸ How are the administrative systems working?

> ▸ Is the learning program operating on budget and on time?

> ▸ Is each of the initiatives supported adequately?

> ▸ Have trainers been prepared?

> ▸ Is the vetting process for outside vendors resulting in reliable selection of good lunch-and-learn sessions?

> ▸ Are the evaluation methods giving us reliable feedback?

> Have the frequency and content of EDCOM's progress reports addressed people's questions and concerns?

> Have our recognition and marketing initiatives attracted a cross section of the firm's members to the program?

The kinds of basic data that firms find useful for responding to such questions include the following:

> Number of learning events available

> Number of HSW sessions or hours available

> Percentage of employee participation.

> Average number of hours completed per employee

> Average number of events attended per employee

> Average cost per employee

> Average scores on seminar evaluation forms

Most useful to the firm are data that are tracked over years to identify trends. For the last three years, has the percentage and number of participating employees gone up? Has the average cost per employee dropped? Is the trend for budget adherence improving each year? After the number of learning events has leveled off, has the relative mix of events—including individual initiatives, research projects, study tours, and the like—become better balanced? From the very beginning, the firm must benchmark information about the professional development system for comparative purposes as the program evolves. Even more substantial benchmarking will occur to track the learning that people actually do.

Evaluating Learning

Of the five elements of a professional development program, evaluation (Figure 9.1) is the easiest and most satisfying, because it responds to all the work that has already been accomplished—assuming that the elements were, in fact, addressed in order.

Alas, of course, some firms begin offering continuing education events (implementation) without having a strategy and/or without the benefit of an assessment of learning needs and opportunities. In the absence of those elements, the evaluation process becomes much more difficult, because suddenly the firm has to decide what to evaluate and how to benchmark. Not surprisingly, firms that don't address the first two elements by the time they reach the evaluation state typically decide to do so immediately thereafter.

For design firms, the evaluation of learning spans four levels, from microcosm (How did people like the event?) to macrocosm (How has the firm's prac-

☑ **Key Point**

For design firms, the evaluation of learning spans four levels, from microcosm (How did people like the event?) to macrocosm (How has the firm improved as a result of the entire professional development program?).

Figure 9.1 The evaluation and improvement element.
© 2002 Blackridge, Ltd.

tice improved as a result of the entire professional development program?). The first level is participant engagement, through which the firm gathers participants' personal reactions to the event at the time. The second level, short-term participant performance, measures learning that is observable through tests prior to and immediately following the event. In NAAB terminology, this kind of retention would reflect the "be aware of" or "understand" level of comprehension. The third level reflects long-term participant performance and the NAAB "be able to" level of application to practice. Firm performance assesses the degree to which participants' knowledge building stimulates long-term improvement to the firm itself.

As Chapter 4 explained, professional development events are designed around learning objectives, so evaluative questions and processes test achievement of the stated learning objectives, at a minimum. For example, in a Gresham, Smith course called "Supervisory Skills Training," learning objectives included:

➤ To make supervisors aware of employment laws, from hiring an employee through termination.

➤ To acquire skills and tools for improving employee development and job satisfaction.

➤ To improve interpersonal and coaching skills.

When it came time for evaluation and benchmarking, Gresham, Smith studied the impact of the course through all four evaluative levels:

➤ End-of-class evaluations, to determine relevance of material, as well as level of engagement.

➤ Employment law pre- and post-tests, to measure short-term learning, as well as to reinforce important points.

> ▶ Participant self-evaluation survey, 90 days later, to determine applied learning.

> ▶ Benchmarked staff turnover rates, record of timeliness of performance appraisals, and specific exit interview queries, to track improvements in the firm's long-term performance in supervisory skills.

The more critical the knowledge or skills, the more evaluative levels should be used to determine, and to reinforce, retention and application to practice.

Level 1: Participant Engagement

An evaluation form is the simplest and most efficient medium for obtaining information about participant engagement in, and satisfaction with, learning events (see Figure 9.2). A written—paper or online—evaluation process requires several things: incentive for busy people to complete it; participant anonymity to encourage candor; simple format and clear directions to expedite both completing the survey and studying results; a combination of closed and open questions to invite feedback; and generic and consistent format for similar in-house events that will help people move through questions quickly and respond accurately.

Questions are simple, and they touch on content, speaker effectiveness, and learning formats, as well as relevance to participants' jobs. For design firms, one powerful benefit of an in-house professional development program is the increased communication and understanding among employees outside the crush of project work, thus the question about networking.

Figure 9.2 is a one-size-fits-all form that is very useful for evaluating and comparing events provided

Key Point

Participant satisfaction forms are the most basic feedback instrument; they are the cornerstone for program evaluation and can be designed to reinforce learning, as well.

Event:						Date:

Please rate the session on a scale of 1–5; 5 is outstanding.

Overall content	1	2	3	4	5
Speaker knowledge	1	2	3	4	5
Speaker presentation	1	2	3	4	5
Handouts	1	2	3	4	5
Visuals and samples	1	2	3	4	5
Q&A opportunities	1	2	3	4	5
Small group activities	1	2	3	4	5
Individual activities	1	2	3	4	5
Networking opportunities	1	2	3	4	5
Achievement of stated learning goals	1	2	3	4	5
Applicability to my work	1	2	3	4	5
Overall value of this program:	1	2	3	4	5

Do you have any suggestions for improving this session?

•

•

Name (optional):_____

Figure 9.2 Basic evaluation form for an event.

by outside vendors and consultants. The same form could be used across the board for in-house seminars and courses, but the advantage of such a practice is also a disadvantage: People become so familiar with a generic format and questions that they expend less and less effort completing and, thereafter, compiling and studying the results.

A better way to assess proprietary events is to combine consistent format with queries particular to the event. The form in Figure 9.3 is a simple format with repeated criteria, but specific topics and learning activities are culled out of the actual content for feedback.

Simple evaluation processes in themselves reinforce learning to a degree, merely by causing people to reflect on the event; and a small addition to a form can increase retention further. The chances of someone retaining and using ideas presented in a seminar increase dramatically if that person writes down actions he or she could take to implement ideas into daily work. Fully aware of this educational tenet, Rosser International builds into its evaluation process a question that stimulates learners to move toward implementation. The question: "Name the job-related behaviors or skills that you will change as a result of this experience."

Firms typically have various forms and processes, each to evaluate a different kind of event or activity. Some consistency among all of them is desirable, primarily for the sake of reliability. For example, if a firm uses both the forms in Figures 9.2 and 9.3 at times, the fact that both use the number 5 as their "outstanding" score would increase the odds of people rating elements as they intend. Had one of the forms used the number 1 to represent excellence, chances are that many of the participants would assign ratings opposite from their intentions. Similarly, if a firm were to use both forms, it would be wise to list the number ratings either as ascending on all evaluation forms or as descending on all.

Course: Introduction to Project Management

Circle the rating that best describes each segment, using the following key:
5 = Outstanding <----------------> 1 = Poor

The Written Word: Contracts and Promises

Overall content	5	4	3	2	1
Materials	5	4	3	2	1
Presentation	5	4	3	2	1
Usefulness	5	4	3	2	1

The Art and Science of Project Plans

Overall content	5	4	3	2	1
Materials	5	4	3	2	1
Presentation	5	4	3	2	1
Usefulness	5	4	3	2	1

Developing and Refining a Scope of Work

Overall content	5	4	3	2	1
Materials	5	4	3	2	1
Presentation	5	4	3	2	1
Usefulness	5	4	3	2	1

Case Study: Developing a Staffing Plan for Winton School Renovation

Overall content	5	4	3	2	1
Case study team	5	4	3	2	1
Usefulness	5	4	3	2	1

Schedule Development and Management

Overall content	5	4	3	2	1
Materials	5	4	3	2	1
Presentation	5	4	3	2	1
Usefulness	5	4	3	2	1

Roles, Responsibilities and Clear Assignments

Overall content	5	4	3	2	1
Materials	5	4	3	2	1
Presentation	5	4	3	2	1
Usefulness	5	4	3	2	1

Case Study: PM as coach on the MetroWest Project

Overall content	5	4	3	2	1
Case study team	5	4	3	2	1
Usefulness	5	4	3	2	1

Budget development and management

Overall content	5	4	3	2	1
Materials	5	4	3	2	1
Presentation	5	4	3	2	1
Usefulness	5	4	3	2	1

Please provide additional comments and ideas on the back of this sheet.

Figure 9.3 Simple, customized evaluation form for an event.

Evaluation

To probe participant engagement in, and reaction to, a learning event, the firm may decide to obtain feedback from a select cross section of attendees, rather than survey all of them. Inviting fewer people to take more time occasionally to provide insights yields different kinds of information. If participants are assembled as a focus group, reviewers can solicit suggestions for improving the event, in addition to identifying strengths and weaknesses.

In terms of measuring how people liked a learning event, firms are wise also to solicit feedback from the expert who facilitated the event. Gresham, Smith and Partners asks facilitators to complete their own evaluation forms for programs they conduct. Questions include:

> Do you feel that you were well prepared for today's class? If yes, evaluate what you did well to be prepared. If not, why?

> What worked really well today?

> What did not work very well today?

> How was class interaction today?

Evaluation forms and processes are not confined to seminars and courses. Chapters 6 and 7 suggested ways to evaluate lessons learned processes and mentoring relationships. In all cases participant engagement may be the most basic level of feedback about the efficacy of a professional development event, but it can be queried in insight-provoking ways. And it is the cornerstone of any proprietary program.

Level 2: Short-Term Participant Performance—Pretests and Post-tests

One technique that design firms use to evaluate individual learning during an event, and to promote retention of seminal points, is to conduct pre- and post-tests or surveys.

In the test version (see Figure 9.4), participants' knowledge of content matter is tested before the event; then the expert presents the session, after which the same test is administered again. Evaluators note the areas in which novices learned the most and least. And participants learn more than they would have without the tests. Simply by answering a list of short questions at the beginning of a session, participants are alerted to important ideas, hence are likelier to recall them. The initial annoyance of knowing less than one had assumed, then participating in the

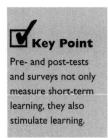

Key Point

Pre- and post-tests and surveys not only measure short-term learning, they also stimulate learning.

Greening of Division 7
Pre-test

1. Define sustainable design and how it applies to green roofing.

2. List four benefits of a green roof system.

3. What is the difference between intensive and extensive green roof systems?

4. List five components of a green roof system.

5. What types of membranes are common in green roof assemblies?

6. What is the FLL?

7. Which code authorities have requirements in place for green roof systems?

8. What is the maximum roof slope in which a green roof system can be installed?

9. What type of roof decks must be used to allow for application of a green roof?

10. What is the most common type of vegetation used for green roofs? Why?

11. How much R-value is added to a structure that is attributable to a green roof?

12. What is the most important element of a green roof assembly?

Figure 9.4 Pre- and post-test on the topic of green roofing. ©Building Logics, Inc.

learning event, then acing the "test" at the seminar's conclusion all combine to effect some improvement in people's performance, at least for a short time.

In the survey version (see Figure 9.5), participants themselves are asked to assess their knowledge, first prior to the event, then afterwards.

Another technique for obtaining feedback about people's learning is to survey participants after they have had a chance to apply new ideas to practice. The Energy Center of Wisconsin (ECW) is a nonprofit consortium that conducts research and provides information and educational programs about energy conservation. A two-time AIA/CES Award for Excellence winner, the Center sometimes conducts follow-up surveys three to six months after an ECW session to find out if participants actually do things differently based on their educational experience. For example, after a course on an alternative approach to lighting,

---

Energy Codes 101

On a scale of 1–5, please indicate your knowledge about the topics covered in this course prior to your attendance, and then at the conclusion of the course. 1 = little or no knowledge.

KNOWLEDGE ABOUT	BEFORE	AFTER
ASHRAE		
Tristate energy codes	_____	_____
Affected structures	_____	_____
Compliance types	_____	_____
Electrical systems and equipment	_____	_____
Mechanical systems, service systems, and equipment	_____	_____
Thermal envelope	_____	_____
Code check processes	_____	_____
References and in-house experts	_____	_____

Name _____

Figure 9.5 Pre- and post-survey of energy codes.

Evaluation

called Cool Daylighting™, ECW asked learners if they had approached at least one project differently as a result. Feedback like the following indicated that a significant percentage of respondents had looked differently at certain design elements because of their experience in the event:

Design element	*Respondents approaching a project differently*
Window placement	70 percent
Characteristics of glass specified	65 percent
Amount of installed electricity	65 percent
Use of shading devices	57 percent

Surveys and tests following an event are useful not only to evaluate the effectiveness of the activity, but also to promote retention by participants.

Level 3: Long-Term Participant Performance

Regardless of the learning method—seminar, lessons learned, mentoring, individual initiative—the desired result is the same: People will do things differently as a result of their growing knowledge. In design firms, evaluating the degree to which people do things differently means talking to managers and observing work practices, always with the express goal of improving the firm's learning program.

Key Point

In design firms, evaluating the degree to which people retain and apply what they have learned means talking to managers and observing work practices.

It is essential to keep in mind, however, that sometimes the reason learners don't seem to apply their new knowledge, particularly from a classroom event, has nothing to do with quality of the seminar or learners' desire to benefit from it. Sometimes people try out new approaches incrementally, in a way that is invisible to others at first. Frequently, people encounter barriers to new approaches: Innovations may be too costly for current projects. Project leaders or clients may be reluctant to test new ideas on their projects. The leaning curve involved in implementation, and the time needed to recover in case the technique isn't a good match for the project after all, are daunting considerations. Frustration and inertia may also discourage a novice from practicing what was preached. If resources or support are unavailable after the event, and people can't practice the technology or technique, they lose confidence and patience when they try to apply it later. And some learning events, like study tours and research projects, may be so engrossing that their conclusion leaves participants feeling temporarily isolated and bored.

With forethought and planning, most such impediments can be mitigated. And for the purposes of evaluation, reviewers must focus on information that will help enhance professional development methods.

One technique for measuring the long-term impact of learning on participants is to observe their job performance. For example, after a program on project management, Gresham, Smith and Partners conducts random audits of participants on the job, to understand the degree to which PM processes and approaches are being followed. The course is then refined to address topics that are not transferred effectively to work activities. As an alternative to audits, some firms survey project and department managers about their observations of improved staff performance following specific seminars or learning initiatives.

Another technique is to tap the employee performance appraisal process for insights to the effectiveness of the firm's professional development program. When a review indicates a need for improvement or an opportunity for growth, the following year's review will directly measure the benefit of the employee's learning activities during the year. From a broader perspective, questions like "What are your professional goals?" and "What kind of professional development initiatives and programs will help you achieve them?" may point to new learning initiatives for the firm to pursue. The following year, asking "What professional development activities helped you progress toward your goals this year" solicits feedback about the firm's program.

A successful evaluation process is one that provokes new approaches and spurs continuous improvement in the firm's professional development enterprise. Even established programs merit rethinking and refreshment. RTKL developed an in-house university, focusing on courses for improving staff skills. Once it was established, the firm was ready to expand its continuing education program and to embrace coaching, mentoring, and other approaches. The firm recruited an architect with academic experience to lead the transition, and has since identified four themes: growth, dialogue, tools, and exploration. *Growth* refers to expansion of the current program. *Dialogue* addresses exchange among people within and without the firm through symposia, design reviews, and the like. *Tools* means support materials such as the library and an intranet for sustaining the new program. And *exploration* is about contact with the external world through research, links to academia, and other ventures. Such an expanded perspective also merited a different identity.

Insider John McRae, FAIA: From "University" to "Forum"

John McRae is vice president, Education and Training, RTKL Associates, and former dean of the School of Architecture, Mississippi State University. Spearheading the design and implementation of RTKL's broadened learning enterprise, McRae determined that "university" was an inappropriate term and that more accurate nomenclature was necessary.

According to some reports, there are as many as 2,000 corporate universities now in the United States. Corporate education is exploding, rapidly becoming a major force in shaping the direction of adult education in this country. Many, if not most, of these corporate programs are called "university" for example, Dell University, Intel University, Hamburger University (McDonald's Corporation).

The RTKL program, too, was originally called RTKL University. In the fall of 2001, with plans for a greatly expanded education program under way, we decided on a name change, for several reasons. There was a strong desire for a program name that would reflect a broadened emphasis, beyond the excellent but limited range of courses that had previously been offered.

The word "FORUM" embodies a wider set of educational intentions, placing emphasis on the notion of dialogue and active learning contained in Webster's Dictionary definition: "assembly for the discussion of public matters or current questions." FORUM is intended to address issues of firmwide interest, as well as directions in education and the design professions, thus connecting with the spirit of the program's tagline: "FORUM: An Open Curriculum for RTKL." FORUM is therefore seen as an integral part of the firm's culture, connecting to all staff levels and across all disciplines. Another reason for the name change is perhaps more difficult to explain.

One of the goals of FORUM is to develop strong collaborations and partnerships with universities and, as such, there is a reluctance on our part to refer to our own program as a "university." RTKL seeks the energy and spirit of vitality associated with universities while at the same time identifying with the realities of the corporate realm.

A final reason for the name change is that FORUM is easy to say, and students, instructors, managers, and principals may use it as a verb, noun, or adjective, thereby encouraging the integration of the word in the firm's office culture.

In the final analysis, FORUM seeks to meet the professional and personal development needs of the staff in a special collaborative way. The individual who is a student in one area may be a teacher demonstrating expertise in another area. This symbiotic relationship, sustaining a "bubble-up" level of energy, keeps the prospect of learning fresh and alive.

Level 4: Firm Performance

The fourth level of program evaluation is firm performance. The underlying motive for instituting a proprietary professional development program in the first place is to enhance competitive edge in the marketplace, so evaluation of the program is not complete until it studies impact on practice.

Key Point

Benchmarking requires recording data prior to institution of the firm's program, and then consistently tracking it over time.

Benchmarking is a meaningful way to track the degree to which the learning program is stimulating long-term improvement to the firm. To this end, a firm tracks progress on reaching its strategic goals, as described in Chapter 2, and on filling the needs and seizing the opportunities identified during assessment (Chapter 3). Benchmarking requires consistent evaluative criteria, reliable measurements, accurate record-keeping, and a great big grain of salt.

The salt is important, because, in many ways, development of design professionals is so closely intertwined with every other aspect of work that firms have considerable difficulty isolating the precise cause and effect of quality improvements and performance enhancements. Is the fact that I have become a better PM today the result of a great PM course, the fact that I have been working with a hands-off PIC and have benefited from her trust and my autonomy, or that I have been reading some very helpful books? Maybe I am just lucky enough to have great communication skills.

Thus, benchmarking. Firms that have tracked multiple trends over time, starting before the learning program was in place, are comfortable with the information they have accumulated and its relevance to the performance of their learning programs. One of the reasons that FreemanWhite invests 4 percent of its revenues in professional development is that over three years in a very good market it observed turnover decreasing from 14 percent to 8 percent. In the same time frame, profitability increased 4 percent in spite of the expense involved in starting the multi-faceted program.

Turnover and firmwide profitability are meaningful benchmarks for most firms that want to understand how their program is contributing to practice. Average budget performance on projects, errors and omissions (FreemanWhite's declined), and insurance rates are signals for design firms. Other commonly tracked statistics focus on staff accomplishments like the following:

> Number of professional licenses and certifications held by employees.

> Percentage of staff passing state or association registration or certification exams.

> Percentage passing on their first try.

> Number of staff members who meet their professional association's continuing education requirements through the firm's program.

> Number of staff who are LEED-certified.

Increasingly, design firms look to trends in the feedback received from client satisfaction surveys that may be conducted every two or three years. And the program may deserve part of the credit if the firm observes an increase in "good" clients, specifically those that inspire staff to do their best work and whose definition of quality matches the firm's.

Reliable evaluation processes tell a firm if it is investing its professional development resources wisely, where it should make future investments, and how it should improve the program to reflect the firm's evolution.

Mavericks and Sole Proprietors

As RTKL has done as a firm, an individual can modify his or her learning strategies to reflect evolving personal passions and changing client priorities. Interests and priorities change, and so do some success criteria. For Peter Vanderwarker, Honorary AIA, the over-riding goal is always client satisfaction. But along the way, he adopts additional success measures for himself, depending on his current passion.

Insider Peter Vanderwarker, Honorary AIA: Learning over Time

Evaluation involves taking stock of what you do and then determining how to improve. Peter Vanderwarker is an award-winning architectural photographer and author of five books. His work appears regularly in the architectural press and his photographs are in the permanent collection of the Boston Athenaeum and the MIT Museum. One of Vanderwarker's success measures is the degree to which his knowledge and skills help his clients achieve their aspirations.

Architectural photography is not hard to learn. Good photographs go on the wall, bad ones go in the trash, and the professional photographer should learn the difference quickly in order to survive.

The more difficult task is to invent a strategy for deliberate learning over one's career, in order to expand the ways that your work can be used by others.

The best learning strategies are ones that integrate your own interests with those of your clients. Spending significant time and effort defining these interests is a great investment. Learning how to manage time is a must.

At the beginning of my career as an architectural photographer, I had little work, lots of time, and an interest in the architectural history of Boston. At the Boston Public Library, I found an excellent collection of historical photographs, and after two years of work, found a publisher for my first book, *Boston, Then and Now* (NY: Dover Publications, 1982). Although I made almost no money, I learned an enormous amount.

Robert Campbell, FAIA, the architectural critic for the *Boston Globe*, wrote a foreword to the book, and I suggested that we collaborate on a series of photo essays called "Cityscapes of Boston" for the *Boston Globe Magazine*. The series has been running continuously since 1983, and is one of the more popular regular features of the paper. "Cityscapes of Boston" became a book in 1992, published by Houghton Mifflin.

Everyone needs some sort of time-out at mid-career. After about 15 years of photography, I began to feel stale and in need of a change. I was fortunate to discover an extraordinary learning program at Harvard University for mid-career professionals in the design fields. The Loeb Fellowship allows a group of about 9 or 10 to spend a year at Harvard: attending classes, participating in seminars, sponsoring dinners, and doing independent studies. It provided me with a stimulating learning environment to try something I had not ever done—writing.

A year at Harvard is not the only way to access learning situations. Most often, valuable learning resources are right under one's nose. My clients are a very skilled and knowledgeable group of professionals, and I am not afraid to ask them for help on projects that I am working on. Recent projects include books on the gardens of Beacon Hill, Boston's Big Dig, and Trinity Church in Copley Square.

Architectural photographers, like architects, want to think that their work will make them immortal. For most of us, this isn't true, but it is still a good way to operate. Our work is as good as the ideas that we care about. Continued learning makes our professional work more interesting to ourselves and more useful to others.

©Peter Vanderwarker

Mavericks and sole proprietors may evaluate their development in many of the same ways that firms do. In addition, individual professionals might consider the following:

> What have been the most interesting and provocative sources of personal and professional growth this year?

> Where am I in terms of the benchmarks (some of which were identified in the quiz in Chapter 2 for mavericks) I set for my personal and professional growth and satisfaction?

> In what kind of projects or roles should I be involved in the next 12 to 15 months to continue my development?

Of course, introspection sometimes leads to a change in direction. Doing things differently can become doing different things, but both are the goals of learning. And learning from learning is the subject of the next, and last, chapter.

Learning from Learning

All five elements of a professional development enterprise are in place. The firm has set educational strategy based on its long-range plan. It assessed learning needs through various means. It has planned, designed, and implemented an array of appropriate knowledge-building initiatives. And evaluative information has helped its educational program to be even more effective.

But the loop is not closed until knowledge generated through the educational program helps mold strategy and shape the firm itself (see Figure 10.1). New perspectives unearthed in mentoring relationships, questions raised through the in-house curriculum, lessons learned from projects, and many individual and ad hoc initiatives spawn new opportunities for the firm's evolution and development. The purpose of the learning endeavor is not knowledge for the sake of knowledge; it is knowledge for the sake of honing competitive edge. Leaders of the firm must consider the implications of what the learning process reveals, not just about the firm's educational activities, but also about the firm and its long term plan.

Figure 10.1 Closing the knowledge-building loop.
© 2002 Blackridge, Ltd.

Learning for Competitive Advantage

As was discussed in Chapter 1, competitive edge is about distinction. A proprietary professional development program advances the firm's distinct attributes by feeding the firm's accumulation of knowledge, stimulating business excellence, inspiring innovation and fresh ideas among its staff, and reinforcing the firm's culture.

The continuous *accumulation of knowledge* through various and varied learning approaches—traditional "classes," coaching relationships, and lessons-learned sessions, mentoring relationships, and individual initiatives—stimulates:

➤ Research and analysis activity within the firm

➤ Intellectual legacy from generation to generation

➤ Continuous and thoughtful study of the client world

► Transformation of the project delivery process into a learning lab for all team members

To close the loop, the firm employs the information it accumulated through its professional development program to question how well it serves clients, community, and staff, and to suggest improvements. Should the firm adjust its client service methods in response to information uncovered through the lessons-learned process? Do trends identified through research and individual initiatives point to new markets for the firm? And has a mentoring relationship suggested a new spin on an old technique that others should test?

Stimulation of *business excellence* results when the firm's learning process informs and enhances its performance as a business. To close the loop, the firm looks to the professional development program for new questions about how effectively the firm operates. Have lessons learned pointed out weaknesses in the firm's quality control process? Have evaluations from certain courses suggested that the firm's approach to setting fees undermines the ability of project managers to control costs effectively? Have the results of seminars in presentation skills indicated that the firm underestimates staff understanding of, and capabilities in, marketing?

Innovation and fresh ideas are created when a learning program inspires people to pursue alternatives, question status quo, and push for change. Closing the loop means asking questions about where the firm is going. How effectively does the firm identify, assess, and adopt innovative ideas that will prepare it to be viable in the future? Have data from lessons-learned sessions shown that the firm needs to consider abandoning a market that is evolving away from the firm's skills? Has information from vendor lunches indicated that the firm should modify some of its project approaches or design standards? Have answers about professional goals on the annual review forms indicated that seniority should no longer be the primary criterion for promotion?

By instituting a learning program, a firm is committing to the protection of its heritage and the reinforcement of its *culture*. It is saying that its basic values and personality must continue within the context of a changing business environment. Closing the loop means questioning what the firm has historically held dear in light of new information and insights. Has the new project management curriculum resulted in a different attitude about authority and responsibility in project roles? Have the results of some mentoring relationships pointed to growing collaboration and information sharing across disciplines? Does the format of different lessons-learned sessions reflect dissonance in the way the firm serves clients?

Learning Hard Lessons

Sometimes a lesson that the firm learns from its professional development program is not one it might have chosen to learn. For starters, there is a lesson about the risk of launching a learning enterprise.

Consider, for example, the situation of a principal of a 150-person architecture and engineering firm. Reflecting on his firm's experience in instituting a program, he noted that people suddenly seemed more focused. They were speaking the same language in a way that they hadn't previously, and they were working well together. Then came a few changes in the firm's senior management. Support for individual professional development and the firm's program dipped. The voices of principal advocates of the program were drowned by the noise of more urgent matters. Within a year, the quality of project documentation eroded, and some errors required costly corrections. Morale eroded, too, and some key staff left. The principal was also preparing to announce his imminent departure. As he explained, "When a firm focuses on individual growth and achievement, everyone is willing to put more into it. When that focus is absent, people's hearts aren't in the firm anymore." Once a program is put in place, it cannot be dismantled without ramifications and loss of much more than the program itself.

Unanticipated lessons can emerge in other ways, too. What if staff seem to resist a program that has been designed expressly for their benefit? Sometimes people are slow to attend courses or to offer to serve as instructors, simply because programs need to be marketed more effectively or because people don't fully understand the connection between professional development and their career potential. But when people are also reluctant to share their experience and expertise with others, or to support the firm's vision for knowledge building, there is probably something systemic to the firm that actively impedes collective learning. If people in a design firm do not value professional development for themselves or their colleagues, it's time to learn an unhappy lesson. The firm has a problem that a professional development program can't solve.

Three Beneficial Lessons

But for healthy firms, learning energizes. Smart people like to stay where they can stay smart. They thrive in an environment where a desire for excellence is supported by a learning system and where change is welcomed. As spelled out on the cover of a recent Gensler annual report: "You can never stand still."

No matter what else design firms discover through their proprietary educational programs, at least two worthwhile lessons seem to accrue to learning firms: enhanced communications and trust among employees, and greater understanding of, and respect for, the design professional's multitextured expertise.

Even in small design firms, communication is often neglected because projects consume all available time. A learning program that incorporates all three levels of knowledge sharing (training, coaching, and mentoring) spurs meaningful communication between experts and novices. Experts share their knowledge first through instruction, which is primarily one-way. Then they work with learners, side by side as coaches, observing and critiquing in more of a shared learning format. Finally, the expert becomes a resource, who offers support and advice to a competent professional. As a facilitator takes learners through the levels and witnesses their development, he or she becomes more confident in their ability. As novices experience greater responsibility, they grow more confident and more autonomous (see Figure 10.2). Both learn better to understand and trust each other's abilities.

The Involvement Model introduced in Chapter 4 reflects the synergy between facilitator and learner

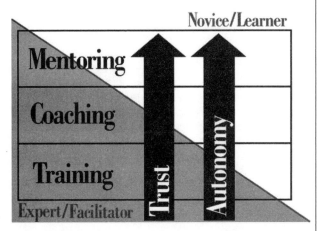

Figure 10.2 Trust and autonomy in the Involvement Model. ©Blackridge, Ltd.

through levels of expertise. Part of closing the loop is capitalizing on the growth participants experience in communication and autonomy through the firm's lifelong learning program. Professional activities should evolve to reflect people's new abilities.

The second basic lesson of a proprietary program is a clearer vision of the range of skills and aptitudes that is necessary in a firm. The more deeply people are involved in the firm's program, the more passionate they become about sharpening all their talents in order to make the greatest contribution to clients and community. Although most programs start in classroom forms that focus on technical skills and the conveyance of information, they evolve into richer programs that address business, organizational, and leadership aspects of professional service. For design firms, and for mavericks, closing the loop also means synthesizing all that one knows and applying it to projects and problems in ways that expand one's work and extend it far beyond traditional design services.

Insider Ambassador Richard N. Swett, FAIA: The State Department Counters Terrorists with Design

A primary goal of professional development is to be able to contribute greater value to clients and community. Some practitioners, mavericks included, demonstrate that contribution in unusual and significant ways. The Honorable Richard N. Swett, FAIA, United States ambassador to Denmark from 1998 to 2001, is a maverick who has tapped his architectural expertise for the benefit of his diplomatic "clients" on several occasions.

On October 31, 2001, a charrette was conducted by the U.S. Department of State to design a system to organize and integrate information from all over the world in the government's fight against terrorism. The system was used to build an anti-terrorism coalition of allied nations against terrorism following 9/11.

Undersecretary Marc Grossman, the director general, had called on me because he was aware that I had used my architectural design experience and design management skills to overhaul the management structure of the U.S. Embassy in Denmark. In Copenhagen, I had introduced embassy staff to a team-based management process, similar to the teams that form around projects in an architecture firm. The difference was that the embassy teams were formed around projects such as issue campaigns and diplomatic dialogues. Instead of using building materials, they used information as their building blocks. Instead of designing office structures, they designed information structures for scheduling and measuring results on complicated, interrelated diplomatic discussions.

This approach caught the eye of Undersecretary Grossman, and, shortly after 9/11, I was asked to assist in designing a solution that could rapidly coordinate handling of the plethora of information being generated amidst the unprecedented crisis.

I suggested that we convene a design charrette, utilizing the skills of accomplished architects as well as computer systems designers. Two firms in particular seemed ideally suited for this emergency, because they emphasize in their client relationships the importance of understanding and designing processes that operate within the buildings they design, not just the building itself. They understand that the flow of information within an environment is as important as the flow of material and people. In fact, one of the two firms, NBBJ, represented by its chairman, Friedl Bohm, FAIA, was talking about expanding into consultation services to help clients design the flow of their business processes. The other firm called in to participate was Gensler, represented by Diane Hoskins, AIA. An architect and an MBA, she understood the benefit of applying the creative problem-solving skills to modern business management practice.

By the end of that October day, three groups of practical recommendations were offered in primary areas of the government's management challenge: (1) top-down leadership action, by priority; (2) bottom-up information capture and sharing, also by priority; and (3) a description of the presentation tool that would facilitate a two-directional flow of information using critical path management technology.

The results: A management team matrix that identified goals to be achieved, and critical path schedules that outlined and prioritized the necessary actions to be taken. With these, the State Department created an effective new working process and developed tools to build order out of a huge and chaotic information database.

The Third Lesson

This book began with a remark from one of the principals of Cambridge Seven Associates, and it ends with the thought of another. In May 2001, Paul Emil Dietrich, FAIA, was about to undergo surgery to treat his cancer. He knew the surgery would be very risky, and he wrote what ended up being his last note to the firm's members. In the note, Dietrich thanked his colleagues for their support, praised the firm's creative environment, and in his conclusion, urged his friends to learn from each other: "Always remember to share your ideas and resources. It encourages better design and enriches life."

Suggested Learning Objectives for *Architect's Essentials of Professional Development*

This appendix contains the learning objectives that I used in developing each chapter of the book. You will have additional or other goals in mind. If you plan to use the book as a learning experience, and to record your activity with the AIA's Continuing Education System in the form of a Self-Report, you must be clear about your learning objectives. You must also track the amount of time you invest in reading each chapter and in completing related leaning activities. Suggested learning activities appear in some chapters. Other activities are listed here. Obviously, none of them addresses health, safety or welfare (HSW) matters.

Chapter 1: Competitive Edge

By the end of this chapter and completion of the suggested activity, readers will:

> ▶ Understand at least four ways that a proprietary professional development program can enhance a firm's competitive edge in the marketplace.

> ▶ Be aware of the kinds of cultural attributes that distinguish design firms from each other.

> ▶ Understand some of their individual competitive attributes.

Chapter 2: Strategy

By the end of this chapter and the activity suggested in "Mavericks and Sole Proprietors," readers will:

> ▶ Understand the five elements of a strategic approach to professional development.

> ▶ Be aware of the learning dynamic that forms among the firm, staff, and clients.

> ▶ Be able to outline strategic learning plans for themselves or for their firms.

Chapter 3: Assessment

By the end of this chapter and the activity suggested in "Mavericks and Sole Proprietors," readers will:

> ▶ Be aware of the Assessment Pyramid and understand at least five ways to determine learning needs and opportunities for a firm.

- ➤ Be able to ask questions that will clarify a firm's long-range strategy and will identify client trends.
- ➤ Be able to identify some of their individual learning needs and opportunities.

Chapter 4: Program Planning and Design

By the end of this chapter and the activity suggested in "Mavericks and Sole Proprietors," readers will:

- ➤ Be able to match learning processes to professional development needs and opportunities.
- ➤ Understand the need to become familiar with adult education trends before developing an in-house program.
- ➤ Understand the Involvement Model and three common formats for knowledge exchange within design firms.
- ➤ Understand the importance of encouraging individual learning initiatives by members of the firm, as well as formal, organized learning events.
- ➤ Be aware of basic guidelines for developing individual learning events.
- ➤ Be able to write effective learning objectives.
- ➤ Be able to develop personal learning plans for their individual professional development.

Chapter 5: Curriculum

By the end of this chapter, readers will:

- ➤ Be aware of the advantages and disadvantages of a curriculum format.

- Be aware of ways to design a curriculum that focuses on the concerns of professionals.

- Understand ways to approach outside providers so that the firm can receive appropriate seminars and events for its staff.

- Be able to create a seminar proposal form to assist in the development of educational events.

- Be aware of the ways that teaching can be a learning activity.

Chapter 6: Coaching and Lessons Learned

By the end of this chapter and the activity suggested in "Mavericks and Sole Proprietors," readers will:

- Be aware of the distinctions between coaching and training techniques.

- Understand the advantages of a lessons-learned approach to professional development.

- Be able to organize lessons-learned activities for project work.

Chapter 7: Mentoring

By the end of this chapter and the activity presented in Figure 7.5, Personal Protégé Plan, readers will:

- Be aware of the distinctions among training, coaching, and mentoring techniques.

- Understand the roles of mentors and protégés .

- Be able to institute a mentoring program within the firm.

- Be able to develop a personal protégé plan.

Suggested Learning Objectives

Chapter 8: Implementation

By the end of this chapter and the suggested activities, readers will:

> ➤ Be aware of the steps required to implement a professional development program in their firms.
> ➤ Be aware of the elements of a budget.

 Suggested Activity

For the learning goals you have already outlined through the previous chapters, establish a reporting system for ensuring that your learning activities are recorded, documented, and reported to the appropriate licensing and certifying agencies, professional associations, human resources groups, and the like. Establish a budget for money and time you will need to fulfill your professional development plans.

Set up a professional development binder that includes this information, and in which you will note learning activities, identify the strengths and weaknesses of each, and, most important, list the ways that you will try to implement key ideas and approaches into your daily practice. Track people you have met who can contribute even further to your professional growth. Every 12 months, review the binder and adjust goals, reporting system, budget allocations, and learning approaches, as appropriate.

> ➤ Understand the kind of administrative and policy decisions necessary for implementation of a professional developing program.
> ➤ Be able to develop an implementation plan for themselves and/or their firms.

Chapter 9: Evaluation

By the end of this chapter and the activity suggested in "Mavericks and Sole Proprietors," readers will:

- Understand the importance of evaluation and benchmarking to the success of a professional development program.
- Understand how to evaluate a professional development program in terms of the firm's performance.
- Be able to develop evaluation forms and processes for determining participant engagement in learning events and for measuring short- and long-term improvement in participant performance as a result of learning events.

Chapter 10: Learning from Learning

By the end of this chapter, readers will:

- Understand the importance of using insights and information derived from the professional development program to change and enhance professional practice.
- Be aware of the risks of embarking on a learning enterprise.

Bibliography

AIA Firm Survey 2000–2002. "Continuing Education at Architecture Firms." Washington DC: The American Institute of Architects, 2002.

Coxe, Weld and Nina F. Hartung, Hugh Hochberg, and Brain J. Lewis. *Success Strategies for Design Professionals: Super Positioning for Architecture and Engineering Firms.* Melbourne, FL: Krieger Publishing Company, 1992.

Daly, Kyle V., and Susan L. Harris. *Discovery: A Search for New Models of Practice.* San Francisco: Advanced Management Institute for Architecture and Engineering, 2001.

de Geus, Arie. *The Living Company.* Boston: Harvard Business School Press, 1997.

Flynn-Heapes, Ellen. "Identity and Expertise: Cultural Archetypes in the Design Professions," *AIA Handbook of Professional Practice,* 13th edition. New York: John Wiley & Sons, Inc., 2001.

Hobbs, Richard. "From 30,000 Feet High to Sea Level," *AIArchitect.* Washington, DC: The American Institute of Architects, March 2001. http://www.aia.org/aiarchitect/thismonth/0301stories/0301marketplace.htm.

———"Innovation Revolution: from Disney Imagineering to Razorfish," *AIArchitect.* Washington, DC: The

American Institute of Architects, April 2001. http://www.aia.org/aiarchitect/thismonth/0401stories/0401C3hobbs.htm.

"NBBJ Continuing Education Program." Columbus, OH: NBBJ Design, 1999.

Peters, Thomas J. *The Professional Service Firm 50: Transform Your "Department" into a Professional Service Firm Whose Trademarks Are Passion and Innovation!* New York: Alfred A. Knopf, Inc., 1999.

Price, Michael A. "Patterns of Change and Learning in the Practices of Selected Oklahoma Architects," www.telepath.com/mprice,1997.

Stewart, Thomas A. *Intellectual Capital: The New Wealth of Organizations.* New York: Doubleday, 1999.

Valence, Jean R. "Practice and Poetics: Balancing the Art and Business of Architecture," Presentation at the AIA Practice Management PIA Conference. Galveston, TX: October 22, 1999.

Index

Administrative system, 181, 185–189

Advanced Management Institute, 15

American Institute of Architects (AIA)

    Firm Survey 2000–2001, 3

    impact on continuing education for architects, 2

    in needs assessment, 64–65

    in program design, 87, 110, 111

American Institute of Architects Continuing Education System (AIA/CES)

    audits, 186

    Leadership Summits, 8, 10

    Provider Manual, 39, 103, 182

    recording and reporting credits, 187–188

    registering with, 182, 194

    source for manufacturer and vendor programs, 123

Assessment

    of individual needs , sample form for, 72

    of learning needs and opportunities, 38–39, 53–82, 181, 184–185

Assessment Pyramid, 55–80, 185

    clients and markets, 60–62

    external signals, 62–65, 66

Evaluation, 181, 203–222. *See also* Investment and
    return
  of coaching, 151–152
  of firm performance, 43–44, 218–219
  by instructors, 211
  of learning system, 203–204
  of lessons learned, 146–148
  of mentoring, 161, 168, 169
  of participant engagement, 207–211
  of participant performance, 211–216
Evaluation forms and samples
  for coaching, 151, 152
  for courses and seminars, 208, 210, 212–213
  for mentoring, 171
Experts, 155, 192–193. See also Involvement
    Model
  supporting, 103, 105, 122–123
  training 122, 181, 189, 195–196
External providers, incorporation into the program,
    123–125, 129–131

FreemanWhite, Inc. (FWI)
  assessment, 57–58, 66, 71
  benchmarking, 218–219
  curriculum, 117, 118
  program design, 101, 103
  strategy, 31–35
  use of job descriptions, 120

Gensler, 139, 169–170
Goglia, Margaret, 77–79
Goldberger, Paul, 49–50

Innovation, 9, 11–13, 225–226
Intellectual Capital: The New Wealth of Organizations,
    7, 8, 65
International Interior Design Association (IIDA), 132
Investment and return, 41–42, 191. *See also* Budget;
    Evaluation of firm performance
Involvement Model, 92–96, 106, 155, 228–229

Johnson, Mark R., 149–150

Kabza, Philip, 126–127
Knowledge transfer and attrition, 5, 7–8

Leadership involvement in professional develop-
    ment strategy, 36, 37–38
Learning Dynamic, 29–31, 54, 141
Learning needs survey, sample form, 74
Learning objectives, 91, 105–106, 141, 206–207.
Learning objectives for *The Architect's Essentials of
    Professional Development*, 233–238
Lessons learned, 140–148, 181, 192–193
Littell, Marcia, 167–168, 169
Living Company, The, 2, 13, 16, 37
Long-range business plan
    connection with professional development, 28–
        29
    as tool for needs assessment, 36, 37, 55–60
Lowther, Thom, 99–100
Lukmire Partnership, 45–47, 193, 194

McRae, John, 217
McLoud, Bonny, 169–170